SUBPLOT

Memoirs of Chicago's
Kungsholm Miniature Grand Opera

Gary Jones

cp

Copyright © 2018 by Gary Jones.

All rights reserved. No part of this book may be reproduced in any form or by any electrinic or mechanical means, including information storage and retrieval systems, without permission in writing from the publisher, except by reviewers who may quote brief passages in a review.

Library and Archives Canada Cataloguing in Publication

Jones, Gary, 1942-, author
     Subplot : memoirs of Chicago's Kungsholm Miniature Grand Opera / Gary Jones.

ISBN 978-0-921845-49-2 (softcover)

     1. Kungsholm Miniature Grand Opera. 2. Puppet theater. 3. Opera--Illinois--Chicago. 4. Jones, Gary, 1942-. 5. Puppeteers--United States--Biography. I. Title. II. Title: Memoirs of Chicago's Kungsholm Miniature Grand Opera.

| PN1972.J66 2018 | 791.5'3 | C2018-905233-3 |

ISBN: 978-0--921845-49-2

Charlemagne Press
4348 Coastview Drive
Garden Bay, BC
V0N 1S1 Canada
http://charlemagnepress.com

For Jessie V.

Front Cover Photograph: Rolfe from *The Sound of Music.*
Courtesy the Cook/Marks Puppet Collection at the Northwest Puppet Center, Seattle, WA

Kungsholm Scandinavian Restaurant, circa 1970. The original McCormick mansion is behind the facade which was added when an extension for the Kungsholm Miniature Grand Opera was built to the right, between the mansion and the taller building.

1

I HAVE TOLD the story about how I became involved with puppets so many times that even to me it has taken on some sort of myth and wonder. In retrospect it seems so miraculous and perfect. Just how did a skinny little black teenager stray from the cocoon of the Far South Side of Chicago, traveling under the river to emerge onto the sophisticated streets of North Michigan Avenue? In my metaphysical Southern California savvy, surely this was no accident and my life is certainly a testimony to that. But where did the impulse begin which led me to the Kungsholm Miniature Grand Opera? When did little wooden people first enter my consciousness? I never saw a live puppet show as a child and those on television in the fifties, *Howdy Dowdy* which I watched but felt indifferent and *Kukla, Fran, & Ollie*, which I glimpsed only in changing the channel, can't seem to have sown any seed.

Perhaps the gorgeous little clothespin dolls I made as pillow ornaments for Mom's bed? I remember them to this day. One clothespin with a skirt of pink, white, or blue table napkins and some ribbons. A lace paper doily if I was lucky. Layers and layers of napkins meticulously positioned and attached. How I came to making them is a mystery but at age ten I knew it was a suspect activity so I stopped.

The germ probably lives somewhere in one of two stories I infrequently share with an audience after the performance. The first, and to me the most lovely because it's kind of a love story, was related to me by my mother on the night before my father's funeral in 1992. It was after midnight and my brother had just retired. Mom and I had always been night owls and we sat quietly drinking tea at the dining room table when she said, "Did I ever tell you about the first date Daddy and I had?" I replied "No" and she said my father had taken her downtown to the Chicago to see a movie. In l939, the Chicago Theater was one of the grandest of the opulent movie houses in the Midwest. The screen feature in those days was sometimes preceded by a live performer attraction and on this night the billing, at least from my perspective, was very unusual indeed. The house lights dimmed, the curtain rose and the wooden ringleader introduced an entire circus – acrobats, tightrope walkers, elephants, monkeys, and clowns, all virtuosos and fabulous and all made out of wood. Mom said neither she nor my father had ever seen a live puppet show before and they both enjoyed it. She couldn't remember the movie that was shown. Needless to say, I sat astonished and staring at my mother. Incredulous, as I had been in the puppetry business for twenty years and she was only just now telling me this.

The second is not nearly as dramatic but still, I think, contributes something on which to lean. Christmas catalogs. Dolls. I can see them to this very day. The catalogs came in the mail, probably from Montgomery Ward and Sears Roebuck. In the toy sections were at least three pages of dolls. After three or four years of asking, I switched my technique and asked for a boy doll – there were always at least two or three pictured. But this too fell on deaf ears and eventually I dropped the request. I look back now and think how enamored I must have been to risk revealing the inner secret whose existence even I was as yet unaware. But when I wrote boy doll on my little list, I'm sure Mom must have known.

So at age sixteen, I took the subway under the Chicago River for the first time. The number one stop on the other side of the river is Grand Avenue which puts one officially on the North Side of Chicago – the fabled Midwestern heartbeat of affluence, power, decadence, art, and bohemianism. I had called earlier to get the address and probably asked where to exit, but when I came up to the daylight streets, I was momentarily confused. This was very alien territory for me and I proceeded with caution and a definite sense of adventure.

At some gut level I knew I was doing the right thing because Mrs. Morphis had told me so. Dorothy Morphis, the gorgeous, funny, and very unconventional divorced mother of four who had six months earlier moved into my neighborhood. For a very short time I was the boyfriend of one of her twin teenage daughters. Mrs. Morphis was an elementary school teacher who cracked very racy jokes to me and her daughters while we helped her grade papers at the dining room table. Her sophistication and hilarious nose thumbing attitude towards life was intoxicating to me as the young artist that by now I had become. She dated wealthy businessmen and travelled in Chicago's black elite, was well read, overeducated, and cultured. It was she who told me about the Kungsholm Miniature Grand Opera. *Aida, La Traviata, La Boheme, Madama Butterfly* – all done with these tiny little puppets! A complete orchestra of puppets, a puppet conductor, a huge crimson gold fringed curtain under an antique crystal chandelier. Reservations a must.

"Oh, Gary Jones," she said, "It's wonderful. You have to go and see this. I know you'll love it." Of course I believed her and so now I was going to find the place and make my reservations in person. Plus I needed to make a trial run alone to make sure I didn't get lost when I returned with my date. To say I was excited and nervous would be an understatement.

Just one door west of North Michigan Avenue, the exterior of the Kungsholm announced its identity as ivory tower cultural fortress by occupying over three quarters of the block between Michigan Avenue and Rush Street. A grand facade, three stories of tailored gray slate punctuated by two twenty-foot opaque, leaded, amber windows and the black lacquered double entry doors masked separate adjoining structures; the 19th Century Leander Hamilton McCormick mansion, and the newly (l952) constructed theater building erected on the site of the mansion's carriage house. Once inside, one was confronted with the silence that so often is the shadow of opulence. This realm was the vision of one Mr. Fredrik Chramer who had purchased the property in l936 and established the miniature opera on the fourth floor in l940. The famous Kungsholm puppets had been designed and patented by Ernest P. Wolff and his mother Esther. Chramer contracted them to bring their puppets to the theater he would complete in l940. This first theater was destroyed by fire in l947, but was rebuilt as a separate structure in l952. When the new theater opened, the Wolffs were gone, though they retained their design patent granted on August 17, 1943. The record shows the application was made on June 22, 1942.

As a youth of nine in his native Denmark, Mr Chramer had received a present of a tiny opera theater from his grandfather, who carved both the theatre and the puppets for him in 1899. Now as an adult, Chramer had recreated the passion of his boyhood. In the process he created one of the most interesting jewels on the cultural landscape of Chicago. He lavished thousands of dollars on each production. The first act cathedral for *Tosca* cost $9,000.00. The costumes were exact copies of famous originals worldwide, all hand sewn. A twenty-five foot marble entrance foyer connected the two buildings. The interior of the four story mansion housed the famous restaurant. Here one encountered specially woven blue and gold carpeting, stupendous crystal chandeliers, the dramatic grand staircase, imported bronze sculptures, priceless paintings, and other decorative antiques. There were four separate distinguished dining rooms, two bars, and kitchen on the first two floors and basement. The third floor was storage and the bookkeeping office, and the huge shell of the ancient ballroom on four eventually became my domain. Here were piled the dusty and fabulous miniature sets of operas no longer in the rep, together with the scene construction shop. Ten years later I would often scurry across the roof of the mansion to enter a small door which led directly into the fly system of the theater three stories above the stage.

The theater was a sumptuous replica of the Royal Opera House in Copenhagen. The orchestra, balcony and boxes held 210 red velvet seats under a frescoed domed ceiling with a magnificent chandelier. Imagine this skinny little black kid walking through the front door and booking a reservation for dinner and the next performance. I did it quickly.

Some days later, on Easter Sunday, I returned with my date. Paulette had no idea where I was taking her but I remember the look of astonishment on her face when we turned the corner and I pointed out the building. She smiled, we both took a big breath and stepped forward. I'm sure we drew some stares but we were both so absolutely enamored with the environment, neither of us felt anything except awe. I remember the food as only plentiful. The Kungsholm presented what was then the most extraordinary smorgasbord in the city, but true to our middle class black heritage, we were very reasonable about the portions we put on our plates. We had arrived for dinner at six o'clock, at seven thirty we were quietly alerted the curtain would rise on the Miniature Grand Opera at eight sharp. Dessert was finished, I proudly paid the bill and we were given tickets to enter the theater.

I was about to witness my first puppet performance and my first opera in the same evening. The usher handed me two programs. On the cover overprinting a black & white photograph of the Kungsholm exterior I read, Madama Butterfly, Puccini. This was further mystery added to the already exhilarating evening. We took our seats, center at about the fifth row. The house lights and chandelier dimmed to black, leaving the brilliantly lit red and gold curtain to titillate. In the darkness, a slow musical commotion ripened into an orchestra tuning their instruments as fifty-two twelve inch musicians rose into view in front of the stage. Fifty-two tiny music stands were illuminated each by its own lamp, with infinitesimally little pages of sheet music falling over the edges of some. Suddenly a follow-spot hit the corner of the pit at stage right and a white haired conductor, looking more like Einstein than Toscanni, made his way center, turned to the audience and bowed. Paulette and I followed when everyone applauded. The maestro did an about-face, raised his baton, and the overture began! I stared. At the last note, the hydraulic pit slowly disappeared and the curtains parted on the first act of Butterfly and my adult future. Of course I knew none of this at the time. I was too enthralled by the spectacle and magnificent artistry of the entire event. The puppets, no bigger than a modern Barbie doll, exquisitely costumed, acting and singing on a stage with a custom-made four story fly system above them with perfectly scaled scenery fifteen to twenty feet high! Every leaf and orange blossom perfectly painted, and every doorway, window, arch, and bridge executed and realized with a precision befitting the Pentagon. An entire theater built just for this purpose. All of this mirrored the inscription above the proscenium, "Not only for entertainment." In retrospect I marvel. And I cry such things rarely exist in today's world.

The opera was presented in an edited version and ended about two hours later. In those days the long subway and bus ride back to our side of town took about 1½ hours. The bus let us off about six blocks from Paulette's house. It was probably almost midnight but still we were both surprised to find Paulette's dad sitting in his car waiting for us. Without a word he ordered his daughter into the car, slammed the door, and drove off. I wandered home untouched by this uncivilized hostility, but enveloped in an aura of images and sounds which would influence me for the rest of my life.

For next nine years I could occasionally be glimpsed in the audience of the Kungsholm. The fact it was an expensive outing combined with my notion it was a place only to be attended on very, very special dates, and then always with a certain amount of reverence and apprehension, kept me from becoming a regular. I probably passed the hallowed portals no more than seven or eight times from the first visit in 1958 through 1967.

In those years I finally grew up. I found myself in college but unhappy and after two years of trying to follow in my brother's footsteps, I finally quit. I worked a non-descriptive night shift at Spiegel's Catalog for a few months, then more fulfillingly as a YMCA teen counselor, and a Boys Club art instructor. My last job, before stepping onto my true path, saw me bent over a drafting table cutting and pasting advertising at a small agency. This was now 1966 and my identity as an artist was pretty much firmly set. The question was the big one. How does one earn a living as an artist in America? A black one at that? Oh well. Never mind. The first thing, I thought, was to get myself a real studio.

In those days the only two areas of Chicago with any reputation for harboring artists were Hyde Park on the city's south side bordering the University of Chicago and, of course, the Near North Side. Near North was the neighborhood extending from the north boundary of the Chicago River up to North Avenue and going absolutely no farther west than Wells Street. It was closed on the east by Lake Michigan and within this two square mile territory one found the nucleus of the city's cultural arbiters and the Gold Coast apartments of the elite money that backed them. It was honeycombed with snobbish galleries, restaurants, designer shops, and … and … coffee houses next door to bars. This was the hot zone of Chicago in the late sixties. Both the original Playboy Mansion and the Kungsholm Miniature Grand Opera were located within these limits.

I had many doors slammed in my face or was condescendingly told why the lease could not be given to me even if I could afford it. So I searched a little further north and miraculously found the perfect storefront on St. James Place. I was no less the romantic then than I am now and the name of the street swept me off my feet. The rent, at $125 bucks, was a bit steep for my salary at the ad agency but the time was right and I hesitated not for one moment. This was my first real studio. A place big enough, the ceiling was 18 feet high, to allow my imagination to soar. What I remember most about it, however, is that it was an icebox. Although it had a gas fired burner mounted over the door, it was woefully inefficient. All heating apparatus underwent the supreme test during a Chicago winter. Yet I quickly adapted to the sharp chill of living in an inadequately heated space and proudly anointed myself as living the life of *La Boheme*.

2

T HE TASK at hand was to create myself as an artist and into this I plunged and thrashed in a fury matched only by my naive dreaming youth. Somewhere in the midst of scattered canvas, paint, carved wood, and glue, I wrote a letter to the director of the Kungsholm asking to interview for a position in their theatre. I wrote two or three more letters to them before I finally got a reply with an appointed date.

I was told to come to the evening performance on such and such a day and then to present myself backstage afterwards to meet the director. I was at once astonished and terrified! By this time I had made up my mind I wanted to pursue a career in puppetry arts. Why else would I write to the Kungsholm? But now they had actually answered and this time I would not be approaching the building as a patron.

It was far too late to back out and so on the appointed day I took the Broadway bus which routed onto State Street and got off at Ontario. The two blocks east to Rush Street seemed longer than ever and when I finally arrived, I stopped dead in my tracks. Stalling for time, I found myself across the street pacing up and down in front of the entrance. But, like all performers, as curtain time neared I tapped some heretofore spring of courage and stepped out. Not onto a stage, not yet anyway, but merely through the front door where I gave my name to the forbidding looking usher who tore a comp ticket in half and walked me to a seat in the royal box! It was a week night and so the theater was only half full, yet here I was sitting in a gold leafed French chair in the best seat in the house for reasons I could not begin to entertain. Yes I was a total wreck and a little bit nervous.

Strangely the production onstage that evening was *Camelot* as it was to be nearly three years later when I arrived and without warning found a closing tonight notice pinned to my locker door. But that's jumping way ahead.

The Kungsholm Miniature Grand Opera proscenium.

I never liked *Camelot*. The audiences always loved it. I disliked the music, the stupid costumes, and the cheap set that had been built for it. But nearly ten years, since my first introduction to the Miniature Grand Opera, it had ceased to be an opera theater exclusively. Popular tastes, which paid the bills at the theater, had caused the Kungsholm management to slowly add Broadway musicals to its repertory. Consequently when I arrived in '67, only five operas remained out of the original roster of twenty-three classical productions. They were *La Boheme, Madama Butterfly, Rigoletto, Tosca,* and the double bill of *Pagliacci* & *Cavalleria Rusticana.* On the last note of *Camelot* and after the puppet cast and the puppet artists had taken their separate bows, the usher came to lead me backstage. I was sweating bullets, as the saying goes.

Backstage at the Puppet Opera was similar (just on a smaller scale) to any other opera house, full of long narrow hallways and black iron spiral staircases disappearing upwards into the shadows above the scenery. The Green Room was one floor under the stage. This is where I was introduced to David, my prospective boss, should I be hired in a position of apprentice puppet artist. As the director, David not only supervised all staff, selected the repertory, and made musical editing decisions, he was also the person who designed and built the fabulous miniature scenery for which the Kungsholm was so famous. This last task would prove crucial to me personally. Later I found out the interview had taken place in the Green Room rather than in David's office for the simple reason he wanted the other staff to meet me before he offered anything. Backstage at the Kungsholm was the same as backstage around the world. One had to be careful. Often times the melodramas of love, intrigue, jealousy, and revenge, which are so artfully and theatrically presented on the stage, rage in reality in the interpersonal relationships of the people performing the art. Born to the greasepaint, David knew this and wanted to gauge everyone's reaction to a potential new ingredient.

Too pretty, too smart, or overly ambitious would automatically engage a thumbs down. The one characteristic David had not anticipated, however, was now smiling at him as he looked up and saw my black face for the first time. Although he was skillful in camouflaging his reactions, others in the room were less so, as I observed them exchanging sly glances. The group into which I was seeking admittance was very close knit. Six in total, they were more like a circus family than cast members in a repertory theatre. All of them except one had been pushing puppets at the Kungsholm for a least five years – some more. They knew each other well and the repertory, puppets, scenery, and physical nuances of their unique environment to minuscule detail. There had been no indication in either my letters or phone conversations with David that I was black. And although I harbored no agenda of being the first black etc., unknowingly this was precisely the part for which I was auditioning. But of course there were blacks working at the Kungsholm, except those were in the kitchen. None had ever applied for work at the Miniature Grand Opera. But here I stood.

The conversation was light.

> "How did you like the show?"
> "I love *Camelot*."
> "Could you see everything from where you were sitting?"
> "I've been here many times and always wanted to sit in the Royal Box."
> "Have you seen the production with 'real' actors?"
> "They couldn't be half as good as the puppets."
> Laughter.
> "When did you first become aware of the puppet opera?"
> "Ten years ago."

A strained silence. I don't remember anyone besides David having anything to say. Perhaps Luis, who spoke with an accent I couldn't pinpoint. Mostly everyone sort of stared at me and smiled wanly or laughed too hard if anything remotely funny was said. Me? I was uncomfortable. But too thrilled to be sitting in the Green Room of the Kungsholm to take much notice.

After a few more pleasantries, David rose to signal the encounter was officially at an end and the usher, who had stayed through the entire thing, was asked to escort me through the dark theater to the front door. "I'll give you a call in a week or so," David had said as he shook my hand goodbye.

Out on the street in the chilly Chicago night air I remember having a kind of feeling I would return. I hurried to the bus stop, well aware I had to make it early to my cut-and-paste job in the morning. I considered myself an artist, but not yet advanced to that station where one quits the nine-to-five to lean on the paintbrush. Not yet.

The callback came in the form of a letter offering me a position as an apprentice puppet artist at a salary considerably lower than I was making at the advertising agency. I picked up my phone, called David and accepted immediately. *Merde*!

The production onstage, when I arrived two weeks later for my first day, was *Rigoletto*. For me this was a good omen because *Rigoletto* was one of the few operas with which I was in any terms conversant. I actually knew and could sing (well..tried to sing) the duke's famous aria. This, my first night under the stage, is still an indelible image.

A staged promotional picture of the understage during performance. Each puppeteer, on a rolling stool, operated a principal character in the opera. The unmanned controls were chorus puppets which were jiggled by whoever was closest when the chorus singing entered the music. Circa 1950's.

But let me explain the phrase "under the stage." In common language, one is on stage. At the Kungsholm, it was literally true one was indeed under it. Explaining this is a bit tricky, nevertheless. Imagine about thirty heavy steel railroad tracks set parallel to each other with about a two inch gap between them. The tracks are forty feet long and form the four foot ceiling of a forty by forty foot room underneath. In other words, the Kungsholm stage was forty by forty feet, and its floor (the ceiling of the space below in which the puppet artists worked) was reinforced steel girders with two inch spaces between each slat. The puppets sat on top of the steel stage with their controls extending down through the two-inch slots to the puppeteers beneath them. Each puppeteer sat on a fourteen inch high wheeled stool and propelled himself understage while pulling his figure with

A view of the actual shadowy realm under the stage during a performance.

him. The artist had a limited view of the stage above him by tilting his head as far back as he could manage. My first month or so was marred by a sore neck. Everyone said I'd get accustomed to the angle, which really meant I'd learn to befriend the pain. I did. Of course I was assigned nothing important for the next year and even when I became a decent puppeteer, getting new parts proved as difficult for me as a newly arrived neophyte hired at the Metropolitan. The scale at the puppet opera was smaller but the backstage politics were every bit as treacherous.

My duties for *Rigoletto* at the matinee on the first day were zero. David told me just to watch and to take in as much as I could. At the evening performance I was given the tasks of moving a few pieces of scenery between acts. This was repeated for the next few days when suddenly, on a Tuesday afternoon, I was asked if

I knew where the ladies in waiting moved to at the end of the second act during the blackout. I said I did and was forthwith given the responsibility to see all eight of them reached their destination in the wings when everything went dark.

This proved a great challenge for I realized I would have to be as forceful as Sean was when he exited the same puppets. The light disappeared and refocused in about five seconds. All of the ladies had to be gone when the next scene began. Sean's method was to grab the first puppet in each grouping of four and to push the other three with a slam down the tracks 'til they stopped with a bang off-stage. I had heard David admonish Sean several times about banging puppets into the wings. Yet there wasn't much time to do anything else. What would I do? My solution was to ape Sean, but rather than send each group independently sailing, I maintained contact with them while pushing them as quickly I could to a halt. No banging noise in the dark! David approved. Sean disapproved. Everyone understage observed. Especially me.

The hours were long. With two performances every day and three on Saturday, we had lots to do. Unlike other theaters in town, however, we did not belong to the union and we punched a clock. We were required to be onstage at 1:00 pm to set the stage for the matinee scheduled to begin at 2:00 pm. This had to be done quickly, especially if one had usher duty that day which required you to report to the lobby in red jacket, and black bow tie when the house opened at 1:30. Now I learned I had actually signed on for three jobs – soon to be four. Each staff artist was at once a puppet artist, a stagehand, and an usher. Responsibilities were rotated, excluding the roles one performed onstage. These, I learned, were competitively won and relinquished with a grudge.

The matinee was over usually by 4:00, at which time the stage was struck but not reset for the evening show. Theoretically one could punch out by 5:00 and not return until the 7:00 evening call. But almost always there were adjustments onstage or under which required attention and work. For me, this was my time to rehearse my manipulation technique. The evening performance was usually over at 10:30 pm. The theatre was completely empty by ll:30 pm and by then I would be too tired to practice anything.

This was my thinking then (certainly not later) and so without fail I commandeered an unimportant little chorus puppet and carefully put him through my routine of a puppet barre. This usually lasted only about an hour because at 6:00, the theatre staff was scheduled to fetch their dinner from the kitchen if we wanted to eat from the restaurant pantry. Unless one ordered filet mignon, all meals were gratis including dessert. Once I became pals with some of the chefs, filet on the side, was not unordinary. This was a dream job indeed. I just wished it paid a little more. But still, "Hey I'm in the theatre!" I was ecstatic.

3

THEN SUDDENLY the wheel of fortune stopped unexpectedly and the ball fell into my slot. David, the director and the man who hired and protected me, was abruptly fired. There is no gloom like a backstage gloom. Enhanced by the theatrical glare and interpreted through the sensibilities of the artistic staff, the calamity was of gothic proportions. As much as I was still pretty much an outsider, I was fairly ignorant of the details of what had actually occurred and the reasons why.

There were two versions. One from David and of course one from management. Either way my trajectory at the Kungsholm would change dramatically and cast a long cheery shadow down my life for many years to come. According to David, he had been pink slipped because he had hired a black to become part of the theatre staff. Management claimed David was being released because he had caused a huge embarrassment to the theatre by scheduling the premiere revival of the opera *Porgy & Bess* and then informing them the curtain on the new production would not go up on the promised date because the set was not yet finished. Meanwhile the box office had already sold out the house several times for this new event. The house could ill afford this kind of irresponsible behavior when the press was beginning to ignore the puppet opera in favor of the real live opera. - the Lyric Opera of Chicago in residence at the 3,000 seat opera house on Wacker Drive.

Whatever the true reason, it was clear David would not be returning to his office except to collect his personal belongings and to clean out his locker. In the Green Room, even the puppets seemed to be in a gloom. Luis was named the new director and for a short time everything seemed to settle down. Shortly thereafter I was called into Luis's office on my arrival at the theater on a Saturday afternoon.

In today's multicultural awareness, Luis was the other minority on the staff at the Kungsholm. He was Puerto Rican, bilingual in Spanish and English while also possessing dense knowledge of French & German. In addition to this, he had enjoyed a short career as a concert pianist in New York City but, unwilling to confront the discrimination rampant in the concert world, had simply given it all up. He had fled to Chicago where his linguistic capabilities and vast knowledge of the classical music canon had made him perfect for his role as assistant director and principal puppet artist. To watch Luis manipulate a puppet was like watching a world famous pianist over the keyboard. His fingers, arm, and wrist coordination were impeccable synchronized with the music and words of the production. It was an incredible vision to watch him so ardently lost in the score with his head tilted backwards at that impossible angle and his feet maneuvering his wheeled stool with the precision of a champion swimmer. No one – well, perhaps Lee G. on a very good night – could make a puppet express the emotion and movement that Luis miraculously managed. He was a genius destined to become an alcoholic.

But on this night, he casually invited me to go with him up to the ballroom on the fourth floor of the mansion. Although I knew this was where the scenery shop was located, I had never had any reason to go up there and so was more than a bit curious when Luis extended his invitation.

We crossed from the theater lobby into the entrance hall of the mansion with its grand curving staircase leading up to the second floor. Here we bypassed the eager diners and elegant black-tied waiters in what originally must have been a kind of grand parlor or perhaps a library. We quickly turned into more pedestrian steps to the third floor. From there into the shell of another royal staircase which emptied onto the dance floor of the ballroom occupying the entirety of the fourth level. Here the ceilings were twenty feet if not more, but with all of the craft woodwork and moulding removed, there was nothing to indicate the former identity of the vast space.

I immediately perceived it was divided roughly in half. One part was filled with a thousand different things from the restaurant. Everything from extra tables and chairs, to steam tables, stacks of white tablecloths, and antique serving dishes. The other side was, to me, much more awe inspiring.

Standing eerily in the shadows were the old and dusty set pieces from *La Traviata*, *Faust*, and *Carmen*. Piled on top of each other and leaning in every imaginable angle were exquisitely carved miniature facades, archways, staircases, balconies, and doors from the repertory of twenty-three operas. Names and act numbers were scrawled across many as were the initials of former performers with dates back into the forties. Because it was decorated totally in shades of decaying blue, I remember the third act of *Carmen* in particular. Indigo blues and blood reds. How magnificent it must have looked under the lights onstage! Like an antique shop, everything smelled old. I was transfixed.

Scattered around the walls and at odd places mid-floor I saw the machines of the wood-workers trade. Industrial saws, and lathes. Sanders, and routers, and drill presses, and what seemed like a hundred hand tools hanging neatly in racks or laid out on the huge worktables. There was new raw lumber stacked high everywhere: 2x4's, 1x2's, ornate moulding, and plywood galore. This was a carpenter's dream.

Luis switched on overhead beams and suddenly the whole scene was illuminated in brilliant white detail. If inwardly I was denying why I was standing here, it took Luis only minutes to unwittingly remind me of the ancient promise I had apparently made. It was really very simple. David had gotten no farther than drawing the plans and ordering the materials for the new production of *Porgy & Bess*. Management still wanted to go forward with the already posted puppet opera season and to negotiate rescheduling for those who had purchased Porgy tickets. When asked about someone to come in and build the set, David had replied they already had someone in house who could do the job. That someone, he said, was me. Luis wanted to know if I wanted the job. A salary raise would, of course, come with the offer and naturally I would still be needed understage at every show. As he turned to leave, he told me to look around the shop and to be sure to turn off the lights when I returned to the theatre. He needed an answer by the end of the week.

Left alone in the gigantic surreal environment, I remember feeling at once a tidal wave of self doubt matched immediately by the sense of a kid set free in a chocolate factory on his birthday. Of course I wanted the job. But could I do the job? This was the real deal. How had I gotten myself into this? Whatever made David think I could handle an assignment this alien? He had visited my storefront studio on St. James but what had he seen there that translated into set designed and executed by Gary Jones? Looking back I can see it was only the rashness of

Kungsholm Theatre in Miniature

PRESENTED BY

KUNGSHOLM SCANDINAVIAN RESTAURANT
100 EAST ONTARIO, CHICAGO, ILLINOIS 60611

PORGY AND BESS

American Folk Opera in Two Acts
by George Gershwin
Libretto by DuBose Heyward   Lyrics by Ira Gershwin

CHARACTERS

Crown, a stevedore	Warren Coleman
Bess, his woman	Camilla Williams
Porgy, a crippled beggar	Lawrence Winters
Sporting Life, a dope peddler from Harlem	Avon Long
Maria, cafe owner	Helen Dowdy
Jake, a fisherman	Eddie Matthews
Clara, his wife	June McMechen
Robbins, a laborer	Irving Washington
Serena, his wife	Inez Matthews
Jim, a stevedore	George Fisher
Mingo, a laborer	William Glover
Frazier, a lawyer	J. Rosamund Johnson
Rogers, an undertaker	Hubert Dilworth
Detective	George Matthews
Coroner	Peter Van Zant

Production designed and executed by Gary Jones
Staged by Luis Tacoronte
Costumes designed and executed by Roy Slocum
Music preparation by David George

SYNOPSIS OF SCENES

ACT I
Scene 1: Catfish Row
 A summer evening
Scene 2: Catfish Row
 The following night
Scene 3: Catfish Row
 A month later
Scene 4: Kittiwah Island
 That evening

ACT II
Scene 1: Catfish Row
 A few days later
Scene 2: Catfish Row
 The next night
Scene 3: Catfish Row
 The following day
Scene 4: Catfish Row
 A week later

Running time of this performance one hour and thirty minutes.
Ten minutes intermission between acts.

For your convenience, you will find the Viking Lounge on the main floor open during intermission. The theater is air-conditioned for your comfort. Smoking is prohibited in the theater building. Fire exits are located to the right and the left of the stage. We regret we cannot be responsible for personal property unless it is checked.

SYNOPSIS OF LIBRETTO ON BACK PAGE

an over-excited kid that prompted me to say "Yes." The task confronting me was way beyond anything in my experience and the result I hoped to produce would be seen in the first two nights by more people than had ever seen any of the paintings or chess sets I was creating in my studio.

The first disaster-tempting thing I did was to inform Luis I would not be constructing the design left behind by David. I would design and build my own Catfish Row. His reply was, "Fine by me. I'm sure you'll bring something fantastic to the stage. "

Now I was experiencing a totally different kind of stage-fright. This was not at all like what gripped my stomach the moment the orchestra hit the downbeat of the overture every afternoon and evening. Nor did it resemble the feeling of no turning back now that accompanied the parting of the red curtain. Instead I felt a kind of never-ending chasm stretching out before me which led right up to the opening night of a new production of *Porgy & Bess* at the Kungsholm Miniature Grand Opera.

It would be announced, even advertised in the newspapers. So what does one do when one agrees to do something he doesn't know the first thing about? One does what those who have gone before him did. In short, I meticulously inspected damn near every piece of scenery in the theatre. Some of the discarded pieces in the shop I even dismantled and put back together. I discovered extraordinary wood joints, and interlocking angles cut by seeming geniuses of the past. How had they done this?

Simple. They knew what they were doing. My next stop was the Chicago Public Main Library. Research. I unearthed every possible photo of every production of *Porgy & Bess* ever done, and was amazed at the different yet extraordinary interpretations of an ordinary slum in Charleston, S.C. With this done, I knew all procrastination had to come to an end and I sat down to draw. Hell, I never did learn how to draw very well. I couldn't show these amateur scribblings to Luis. I built a cardboard model and painted it white. I was outdone and amazed at how professional it looked. And in a forced perspective on top of it. Yes! I was on my way!

Now all I had to do was to learn how to operate all of the strange power tools in the shop. Looking at the router and the Cutawl, I didn't have the slightest idea of how to handle them, much less what function they provided. I would have to learn by doing. And so I did. And had a terrified blast doing it. No one had the slightest idea I didn't know what the hell I was doing. This was an unbelievable circumstance. How could they not know? I understand now that David's word was enough for everyone and what an incredible chance he was taking in recommending me for the job. It has also crossed my mind David didn't really give a damn what transpired at the Kungsholm after he was fired; and although not malicious in intent towards me, he knew it was risky to hand such responsibility to a green kid. Perhaps he figured I'd either sink or swim. I didn't see him again until years later and by then the question was moot.

My allotted time to work on set construction was between the matinee and the eight o'clock show and as long as I could stay awake after the theatre went dark in the evening. This meant my most intense creative work began at around 11:00 pm and having clocked in at 1:00 the next afternoon, I already had ten hours of Kungsholm under my belt. Typically I stayed until two or three in the morning. I loved it. The only person in the entire building complex, besides the ghosts who roamed the mansion after midnight. I usually ignored them. I couldn't afford not to. Besides their presence rarely intruded as long as I remained in the brightly lit area of the workshop. The dim shadows on the other side of the ballroom were a different story as were the hallways and rooms of the mansion as I descended, turning off lights at each level until I finally reached the stop of the grand curved staircase where I paused, took a deep breath and then without looking back, descended them in a race to the front door. If I had ever turned to glance, I was sure I would see the presence I so sharply felt was watching my back. I loved working late, but I dreaded leaving the house. I was not crazy nor did I smoke weed. Believe me. It was thrilling.

So while the ghosts made untoward sounds and glared at me from dark recesses, I merrily and intensely threw myself into doing whatever had to be done to make the deadline for the previews and the premiere. I couldn't have been as naive as I sometimes picture because one of the first things I did before starting on the set was to build an exact replica of the opera stage in the middle of the workshop. This was my act of claiming the space and making it utterly mine. I moved practically everything that was not bolted to the floor, as indeed some of the heavier equipment was.

The stage floor, as described, was like steel railroad tracks set parallel with about a two inch gap between each. These railroad tracks were actually flattened pieces of steel six inches wide. At random intervals were four inch circular openings through which one dipped the controls of his puppet to simulate sitting on a piece of furniture placed next to the hole. The position of these holes was crucial. Many a night we had struggled onstage to position a piece of scenery to synchronize with the dip spots. I was determined there would be no struggle with Catfish Row, hence I recreated every element and flaw on the real stage on my tryout replica upstairs. Luis thought it was a brilliant idea. As I was still operating out of unacknowledged fear, I was merely covering my ass from every angle imaginable. Luis loved the cardboard model and the management liked it so much as to propose putting it on display in the foyer as advertising for the new season. I responded. "I need the model in the workshop to make sure I don't stray from my designs."

And so it was every night for the next three or four months – the ghosts, the model, and me, high above North Michigan Avenue amidst a flurry and whir of power tools, sawdust, and sweat. The tools grudgingly revealed their purposes and different modes of operation. One by one, as different needs arose, I hunted through the space to find an instrument to achieve my goal. Often I had to laugh as I discovered how something I had been doing with great difficulty with one tool could be easily accomplished with another. Imagine, using a band saw to do the work of a router. But these were small things when compared to the miracle that seemed to be happening to me as I constructed my first show.

It never dawned on me that I had undergone an extraordinary transformation. I was doing the next thing needing to be done and since there was no one looking, I felt safe in just stepping out in the direction of whatever it happened to be. Ultimately I knew at some level I would complete the project on time and it was going to be beautiful. I never hesitated over the how factor. That, I suppose, is the gift of youth.

So as the work progressed and the houses and staircases of Catfish Row began to materialize, I began to have lots of visitors. Everyone, I soon learned, was quite curious to see the results of all the activity on the fourth floor. This included not only the expected interest of my comrades in the theatre, but everybody from the kitchen personnel, to management and even the bookkeeper, whose office on the third floor positioned her to witness progress almost daily. As one person after another came up to take a peek and to take their leave bestowing a compliment, I came to realize in some weird way what I was doing somehow represented the life of the Kungsholm. Looking back I can see it did in a very real sense. For all of its grandeur, the Miniature Grand Opera was swiftly sliding downhill. I had boarded a sinking ship. This fact was absolutely undetectable in the impeccably maintained building and the high prices. The clue visibly lay in the new middle class patrons who came to see the Broadway productions and not the operas.

Until recently, the clientele of the Kungshom had been its neighbors who lived in the Gold Coast apartments across the street and down the block. But from the inception of the real opera, the Lyric of Chicago, virtually all of these people had shifted their allegiance. The crowd at the Kungsholm was no longer quite as fashionable. But that was only what was visible. With management's decision to shift the repertory, there also came a tightening of the budget and a not surprising lackadaisical response from the theatre staff. After a few musicals were added, all of the creative activity of the theater was temporarily frozen. A theatre with nothing new brewing in the wings is a dead theater. Consequently my hammering, and sawing, and the smell of paint signaled a symbolic thaw. Perhaps the ship could be bailed out. Everyone's interaction with me was subtly tinged with the conflicted notion that I was some sort of black savior. Existing semiconsciously in the crossfire of all this affected me seriously in two ways. My self-confidence experienced an enormous boost. The interest, excitement, and gossip about the new show was all centered indirectly on me. This was something very new and pleasing. I had not yet come to fear the spotlight.

At the same time, it dawned on me, for the first time, that my creative actions were powerful if I allowed them to flow uninhibited by fear. The problem was, in spite of all this, I was still scared shitless. So midway through the process I experienced a block. I would spend two or three hours in the shop and literally get nothing done. What if someone noticed? Outwardly I was fumbling with the problems of building in a forced perspective. It took me a couple of weeks to uncover the incongruities and imperfections other designers had liberally incorporated into their work. Henceforth licensed, I untied my knots and forced the perspective to creatively exaggerate my point of view.

By now I was so intensely engaged as to resent visitors when they showed up. Time was running out and the project seemed to have an energy all of its own. Even the ghosts were enthralled and distracting me less and less.

4

SIMULTANEOUSLY, while I was building the set, Luis was cutting the performance tape and plotting rehearsals. He didn't have to do any casting for it was non-verbally understood who would be playing which parts of importance. He would do Porgy and Lee would do Bess. Lee George was the prima donna of the puppet opera. And rightly so. His skill with a puppet matched in technique, if not emotional color, the excellence exhibited by Luis. In many parts Lee was utterly flawless. When Lee manipulated a puppet, sparks flew and he laughed understage while doing it. And occasionally winked when he executed some difficult feat that completely bypassed the audience but made us understage swoon. Lee was serious and playful and often commanded his puppet to perform lewd gestures perceived as unbelievable to spectators because a puppet couldn't possibly do such a thing. He sometimes called the puppets big wooden dildos and under the spotlights, during a performance handled them as such. This irreverence drove Luis crazy.

Luis was, after all, the artistic director before he became the artistic director. It was he who was the only authentic music authority in our midst. Part of what had drawn him to the Kungsholm had been the exquisite repertory. His view was, we had to conduct ourselves seriously understage in order for the puppets to communicate any degree of emotional life onstage. He said it was a very delicate thing we were doing. He could sit out front during a performance and tell if someone was unfocused or playing around understage.

Before Luis, I had never heard anyone use the word "mystical" in describing a theatrical event. Martha Graham used to say either the *kundalini* was present or it wasn't. No if's, and's, or but's. Likewise there would be no if's or and's about the casting of Porgy. Rehearsals were sure to be hell and would be scheduled very soon. It was at these practice sessions I would get my most insightful and practical lessons into the magic of making the little figures express their hidden lives. And although I had heard Luis make incisive critiques and engaging remarks about whose puppet had done what, when, and how, never before had every word seemed so detailed towards creating any one particular vision. The vision was how Luis saw the events taking place in *Porgy & Bess*, and how he thought the characters should move to express things the way he saw them. The subtext to all of this centered on the fact that all of the characters were black and all of the actors (puppeteers) were white. Except for me, who, because of my relative inexperience understage, didn't count. In effect, we were doing a blackface production of an American classic. Everybody was very, very sensitive. Luis, however, knew if he didn't impose a clear concept, the production would degenerate into a series of very unfunny and potentially offensive stereotypes. I got the feeling my silent presence was echoing very loudly.

As each rehearsal period got more and more heated, I found I was developing a corresponding touchiness. Although I had heard or read small references to *Porgy & Bess*, it was not until now that I heard and understood Gershwin's mighty achievement. The edited version Luis agonized over only increased my curiosity and I ended up checking the entire recording out of the library. I was enthralled by the music but much less so about the story, and outright offended by some of the characters. In particular, I hated the scene of Lawyer Frazier selling a divorce.

As the weeks went by, Luis saturated us with *Porgy & Bess*. He would have it playing when we arrived at 1:00 o'clock to set the matinee stage and again he would spin the tape decks while we were eating in the Green Room and getting ready for the evening performance. He said he wanted us to know every note and silence of the music to the point of dreaming it. Needless to say, no one was more engrossed in this premiere than me. All of the heightened focus of the emotional rehearsals served to hype up my activities in the scene shop. I was determined my Catfish Row would not just sit in the background like a little ninny. Somehow I would make it speak an elegant language parallel to Gershwin's and reinforce the nobility and universal humanity of the characters. To say I was over-identifying, and much too personally involved, would have been an understatement and at the same time interpreted as a racist remark. Again I asked myself how I had gotten involved in this unreal world so quickly and so deeply?

Gary painting his Catfish Row setting for *Porgy and Bess*.

As the week of truth approached the atmosphere backstage, understage, and in the Green Room grew thick.

Luis had hired a friend to execute the delicate little costumes. I quickly found a friend in Jorge, who consulted frequently with me on the colors of the buildings against which he would be challenged to skillfully and dramatically dress the puppets. At thirteen inches high, a figure sporting blue or green could quite easily disappear against a similarly colored background structure.

The actual construction of the set had taken much longer than anyone had anticipated. This was, after-all, my maiden voyage into scenery construction and I was learning mountains as I proceeded. One of the more daunting tasks was to conquer all of the different power tools in the shop. The two different band saws, two jig saws, one stationery and one hand held. The monstrous table circular saw which seemed too dangerous to even consider using. The hand-held router with dozens of attachments. The table sander. The two drill presses. And of course all of hammers, screw drivers, vises, pliers, and unidentified instruments I was encountering for the first time. My exposure to such machinery was limited to the wood-shop in a local Park District where there was always an instructor to demonstrate. Looking back, it seems a miracle that with my inexperience I somehow avoided an accident. I reordered lumber twice. But as there was still plenty of time, none complained. They merely appeared regularly at the door to make 'oohs' and 'aahs' and then depart. The particular feature of the set drawing this non-verbal praise were the staircases which had grown from two into a fascinating maze of steps crisscrossing and snaking in every conceivable direction around the property.

This the element of the design probably could have benefited from a tad of restraint on my part. But once I had so successful built the first staircase and observed its quirky mystery leading to nowhere, I couldn't resist another, and another, and another. Everyone thought I had planned it that way. No one double-checked the model which contained only the original two stairways.

The painting of the set proved almost as complicated as the building process. To this day I cannot remember who alerted me in an offhand remark that I had to paint the entire front of the set white and the back of it gray before I began applying the scenic color. It certainly jibes with the correct method but at the time, was a fact quite unknown to me. I take the opportunity to thank them here. I guess I was like a big sponge at the time. There was so much I didn't know about the job I was so heroically executing. I was continually amazed at the progress and quality of what was happening in the scene shop.

5

FINALLY change night arrived. This was our slang for what happened between the time one production closed and another opened. It was an incredible ritualized effort wherein we removed the current settings, stored them, and replaced them with the upcoming show. This was a huge undertaking, comparable to lifting and moving six or seven grand pianos. The scenery was very, very heavy. Characteristically it took three or four people to move one set piece. Either up or down a typical backstage spiral stair or maneuvered out over the orchestra pit, carried through the theater and then down a more reasonable stair to the basement. In addition to this, there would be drops to remove and hang in the three story fly system, masking panels to set in the wings, and a plethora of logistical problem-solving attached to the entire undertaking. Lastly the puppet casts had to be switched, and the lighting scheme redone and re-hung. This was all miraculously accomplished overnight. On a normal night with normal catastrophes, we would usually leave the theater around three in the morning and be due back by one the next day. Change night rolled around every two weeks! The one thing that made it appealing and almost something we looked forward to was a backstage tradition called the 'Midnight Snack.' At some point of exhaustion, perhaps around 1 am, someone would yell, "Snack time!"

Whatever one was doing was immediately halted and after dutifully washing our hands like good little boys, we would head for the kitchen of the restaurant. Although the gigantic refrigerators were locked, some enterprising puppeteer had long ago fashioned primitive keys from sheet metal in the scene shop. The director of the puppet theatre kept the keys and passed them down when he vacated the post.

We entered silently and when the lights were switched on, we all let out a yelp as one container after another was opened and raided. Heaps of caviar and stacked slices of rare prime rib were carried back to the Green Room augmented by every exotic concoction that made the famous Kungsholm smorgasbord so famous. On occasion we would not return to the Green Room, but rather turn on the lights in one of the small intimate dining rooms with a grand piano. Luis would sit at the piano where he would play and eat at the same time while the rest of us sat close to him on the marvelous pieces of French period furniture. Needless to say, the dessert refrigerator was everyone's favorite. We needed lots of sugar to get us through the remainder of the night.

It was at the dessert site where I enacted a Three Stooges stunt that would be retold until the place was closed three years later. Desserts were kept in a fridge with three doors; one a walk-in and the others, half doors, one above and one below. Our key unlocked only the upper half door. Someone always had to climb up, jump down into the fridge and open the walk-in door from the inside. On this memorable night, however, when I landed in the dark on the other side, my feet did not hit the floor boards. Instead my socks became quickly semi-wet and cold and I felt as though I had stepped into a mud puddle. I said, "Oh shit!" From without I heard everyone ask, "What's wrong?" When I switched on the lights and opened the door, everyone fell into gales of laughter to see me standing almost knee deep in a huge tub of whipped cream! Thank goodness someone had the presence of mind to suggest I step out of my shoes to avoid an extensive stretch of literally covering our tracks. To this day I am amazed the kitchen staff never once said anything to us about all the missing food every two weeks. And I marvel even more when I think the two elegant upstairs bars always remained untouched by us. Nothing up there was under lock and key. I suspect early on in the development of midnight snack, the theatre staff discovered the complexities that adding alcohol to the raid would have engendered. Change night was far complicated enough to negotiate sober. The dangers would have only been multiplied by a thousand with a glass of scotch, rum, or wine added to the festivities.

Changing over to a brand new production, however, was quite different from an in-repertory change. In-repertory, sets and props were already in the theatre – stored in the wings, or in one of the other spaces provided. It was relatively easy to retrieve them. The obstacle of a new production was getting the new set down from the fourth floor shop, through the restaurant, grand stair, lobby, into the theater and then up over the orchestra onto the stage.

Sometimes smaller pieces could be disassembled and taken out a fire exit from the ballroom and thence across the roof of the mansion to another fire door at the top of the fly loft of the theatre. Luis usually came up early on the afternoon of the change to determine with me what could go which route. Along the way, we would determine if any furniture in the restaurant needed to be temporarily moved to allow smooth passage.

However, what made new changes so different was the attendant anxiety that everything would properly fit onto the stage, and of course the ease with which it could be moved during intermissions and blackouts. None of this could actually be determined until the set was on the stage and we did a run-through. Although my big idea of replicating the stage seemed the perfect remedy, it would still be a game of wait and see.

On change night, before the premiere of my *Porgy & Bess,* we left the theatre the next morning at 5:30 or 6:00 am and returned at noon to find Luis high on a ladder making last minute lighting adjustments. We rehearsed until dinner time and then solemnly filed understage at 7:45 pm. At eight o'clock sharp, the house lights dimmed to half and a voice announced to a full house the Kungsholm Miniature Grand Opera was proud to present its new production of *Porgy & Bess* directed by Luis Tacorante and designed by Gary Jones. With that, the lights went to black and the lone spot came up in the orchestra and the conductor made his way to center, bowed, turned, raised his baton and the overture began. Luis was conducting as only a man with his music education could. On the last bar the orchestra descended, Luis quickly ditched the conductor and picked up his next puppet, and amid audience applause at the parting curtain, commenced to whisper directions in his authoritative but gentle Spanish accented English.

The restaurant had prepared a special post performance gathering in one of the upper rooms, but midway through the show, everyone understage had ceased speaking to each other in a series of controlled rages. None from the theatre staff attended. We took our traditional back-to-reality bows at the end of the performance and that was the last the audience saw of us. In mandatory attendance, Luis made excuses for us and then himself slipped away. I remember it was a very warm night and I got off the bus a few blocks early and walked through whispers and muffled voices in Lincoln Park to my storefront studio on St James

The cast of puppeteers in front of the Catfish Row for *Porgy and Bess*.
l - r: John ?, Rand Bohn, Gary Jones, Lee George, Luis Tacorante, Donald George.

Place. I had successfully completed the first of several chapters of my time spent over the next three years at the Kungsholm Miniature Grand Opera.

By one the next day, everyone was in the Green Room and hurriedly scarfing down brunch while throwing accusations at others to deflect the glare of their own mistakes during the premiere. It was good natured but things were tense and everyone realized Luis was being very lenient and patient. He could have demanded we appear for a 9 am rehearsal but instead had decided to let the matinee ride, note the really serious missteps and begin another complete run through right after the matinee. He was pretty much resigned the 8 o'clock would also be fairly rough but made it clear everybody had to tighten things up in the next day or so. Or else. The threat was clear if unspoken. Or else meant one could be permanently assigned to tech for the duration.

There were no stagehands at the Miniature Grand Opera. To this day I'm unsure how the house managed it, but somehow they kept the union out.

We doubled as the stagehands. As artists, this is where we were really being exploited. This was not community theatre where everyone does everything. We were on Chicago's Gold Coast, North Michigan Avenue doing thirteen shows, six days a week at a high ticket. Corporate greed. Being the prima donnas that we were, tech was not anyone's choice for the run of a show. There was no glamour in it and it was meticulous complex hard work. Drops had to fly out and set structures had to fly in in a split second. Puppets had to be removed from stage left and switched to stage right and placed in the correct track in total blackout. If a character was mistakenly placed in track four, it was a disaster if it should enter on track six. The reason … simple … the set placement created a wall on track four. The doorway was on track six.

The poor puppet literally left the wings and ran into a brick wall. If this happened, it could only be corrected by the tech guy on stage level, the puppeteer understage was helpless. The tech for every show was nothing to sneeze at. Whereas understage, the performers could cover their butts; if one's attention wandered while doing tech, it could cause a performance catastrophe and even bodily injury. During a blackout, you've gotta be razor aware of every person and puppet's whereabouts before you fly in a five hundred pound house. Usually it took one person plus the occasional assistance of someone understage to run a show. Personally I never minded doing tech but stopped volunteering when I perceived some of my fellow puppeteers felt it was all I should be doing.

The competition for casting understage was fierce and some folk were quietly glad when I got promoted to scenic designer. One less person vying for the part they coveted. Or so they thought. My activities up in the wood shop didn't even approach a diminishment of my ardor for the puppets and taking a bow when the performance was over. By this time I was irreversibly infected with what Jean Cocteau famously called "the red and gold disease" – referring to the traditional red and gold main curtain in theaters around the world. And of course the Kungsholm was no different. Not only did it have a magnificent deep ruby velvet curtain with heavy gold fringe, tassels and ropes, the 210 seats were also red velvet! With the glitter of the main chandelier and the fat ass cute cherubs floating in the ceiling who wouldn't want to blow a kiss and take a bow?

In the end, *Porgy and Bess* was a big success and played to sold out houses but management did not extend it beyond the regular two week run of every show. This is where the Kungsholm differed again from the other pro houses in the city. Normally a show runs until the box office begins to falter, at which time the notice goes up on the board. I think someone at the Kungsholm had decided variety was the name of the game and so they kept shuffling the deck. During my entire three years, no production ever ran more than the regular two weeks. It might be scheduled again two months later but never was any one show allowed to wind down. Every fourteen days we struck one show and put up another. In a way, it kept everything fresh and prevented us from falling into the dreaded routine of long running productions. And perhaps, with puppets who are, after all, much less alive than their human counterparts and unable to keep breathing new energy into the show, especially with a recorded sound track, this was probably a wise decision.

The constant change did tend to keep everybody alert, especially as Luis gleefully shook things up with surprise cast changes. He didn't do it often because the plain fact was, he and Lee George were undisputedly the most accomplished technicians under the stage. The rest of us – Lee's twin Donald, Roy, Charles, David, Sean, John, Roger, Randy, and myself – were not nearly as good and operated at different levels of proficiency. So automatically the lead roles always went to Luis and Lee. But logically they couldn't do everything and so the various supporting roles and the occasional lead would be someone else.

For the first year and a half I rehearsed on my own whenever I could get the chance. This was rather difficult as one's performance was music driven and individually we had no access to the sound booth between the matinee and evening show, which was the only time available for practice. So whenever I rehearsed, I had to sing the song in my head or hum it while I wrestled with the manipulation difficulties inherent for that particular piece. Looking back, I am amazed there were no regular practice sessions beyond the standard rehearsal on the morning after change night and the next show scheduled to open that very afternoon. There was no such thing as a class where technique was taught by the two people with the most experience, Luis and Lee.

The Kungsholm puppets were actually fairly uncomplicated mechanisms. A wire frame body was threaded and set with a series of ball joints at the elbow and shoulder of each arm of the figure. The neck sat in a circle of steel atop the shoulders and connected to a single downward rod which was controlled by the operator's thumb. Both hands were needed to animate the puppet. And although it was a basically simple device, the dexterity required to effect the desired life qualities was no easy challenge. Coordination, timing, and musicality were the essential elements needed.

Early on I learned a key ingredient was where one placed the stillness between gestures. When deployed with feeling and skill, it never failed to deliver a live hand grenade at the feet of the audience. It was a ballet performed by one's fingers, similar to playing a flute, guitar, or even the piano.

But with no formal teaching, one learned through careful observance during performance and just maybe asking Luis to show you how he managed a particular gesture that you were trying to catch. Asking such a question of Lee was simply, totally out of the question. He was extraordinarily possessive of his roles and the secrets of his technique and guarded his territory fiercely. He was the prima donna and was not to be bothered. As a rule, with very few exceptions, the group rarely commented on anyone's performance. If any remark was made it always came from Luis. His was the only word that really mattered anyway. The only time I saw Luis blow his top about technique was during the rehearsals for *Porgy & Bess*.

Luis played Crown and of course Lee was Bess. Normally the two of them were sublime onstage together in for example, Rudolfo & Mimi in *La Boheme* or Liza Doolittle & Henry Higgins in *My Fair Lady* ... but in Porgy, Lee just could not get it together. The problem came in the rape scene on Kittiwah Island. Bess and Crown argue and then tussle before he orders her to get in that thicket.

Perhaps because Lee was such a lyrical performer and there was zero lyricism in this stage moment, it threw him off. But whatever, this veteran Kungsholm puppet artist could not master the moment. Luis rolled the tape back again and again and gave Lee instructions over and over. Still disaster. And it got worse and worse. The rehearsal was stuck at this point and the rest of us relaxed our puppets, hypnotized by this gigantic struggle between the boss and the star. It turned ugly with cursing and finally exasperated, Luis gave up and allowed the run through to continue. Of course on opening night everyone was tense as this segment of the opera approached. Needless to say when it hit. Lee pulled it off with style and the tussle between the two puppets was nothing if not sheer violent poetry.

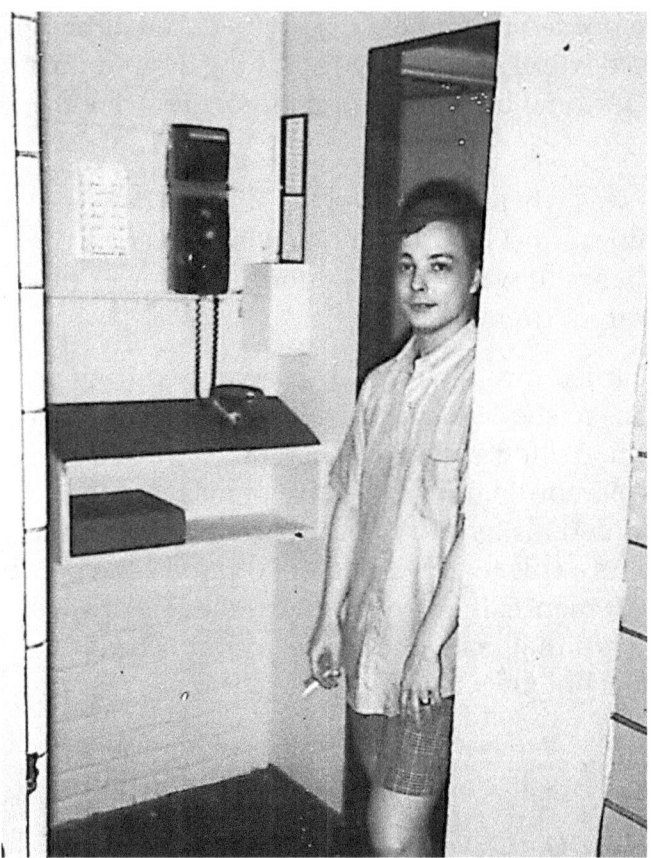

Lee George, the "diva" at the puppet opera who essayed all the leading soprano roles in the repertoire. His talent was magical and we cried during his suicide scene in *Madama Butterfly*. Here he is standing next to the backstage telephone which we often covered with a carpet to muffle ringing during performances.

Afterwards Luis couldn't resist asking why Lee did not deliver in the first place. Lee shrugged his shoulders and disappeared into the locker room. I am confident Lee didn't go off and rehearse the scene alone. During the entire time I was there, I never saw anyone practice anything on his own. I did it constantly because I had to. This was all so new to me and I was absolutely determined I would make a good impression, not only as a worthy artist but also as a black man. Not a day went by when I was not made aware of my singular status in the theatre. I was continuously amazed I was really there. And when my promotion to scenic designer happened, my sense of responsibility to la raza tripled. The only other black people at the Kungsholm worked in the kitchen. The white gloved doorman was white. And when I bowed with the rest of the cast at the end of every show, I almost never saw a dark face in the audience. By extension black faces on North Michigan Avenue in the sixties was an extreme rarity.

Catfish Row with puppets from *Porgy and Bess.*
The photo was taken just before the first performance

A stagehand makes a scenery adjustment before
the performance begins. Note the slotted stage
surface through which the puppets glided.
Circa 1940s.

6

ABOUT five or six months after the completion of *Porgy and Bess*, Luis had a discussion with Tom about the look of the theatre's production of *My Fair Lady*. It was decided the fair lady looked pretty shabby and as it was one of the most popular shows in the repertoire, it needed to be redone.

Actually the opinion probably came from Tom, who operated as the elder among us and was consequently heard and respected. Although he never climbed any ladders, Tom's official position was the lighting technician and he spent most of his time in the lighting booth above the balcony. His knowledge of the opera stage was immense and he had been on staff at the Kungsholm since the early fifties or earlier. He seemed to be about sixty years of age. If anyone knew where the ghosts sat in our 210 red velvet seats, he did. We were all fascinated listening to his stories of the great opera stars who visited backstage with their managers in hopes of making a sweet deal to use their recording of a particular opera on our tiny stage. Their names would be printed in the program and album sales would certainly get a boost. Those were the days when the Kungsholm still retained some of the glamour it held in Chicago's classical music world before the Lyric Opera was founded and began siphoning away audience. Tom was the man out front on whom Luis depended to spot and note when any component of a production was not up to par. Luis couldn't do it because he was always understage performing. The position of stage manager did not exist for us. But fortunately Tom had an eagle eye and came backstage after every show to tell not only Luis, but confront everyone if something was off kilter.

One of his pets was constantly warning against overloading the flash box for the oven explosion at the end of the opera *Hansel & Gretel*. A flash box is an antique stage device used to simulate a big bang on stage. In actuality it was real and dangerous. Tom knew this and had even witnessed accidents. I'd describe it as a metal box one half the size of a shoe box. Its lid was a wire screen with a latch to close. Inside were two electrical terminals across which one attached a single copper wire and then poured about a teaspoon of gun powder over the wire. When one flipped a switch and sent a current through the wire, it, of course, ignited the powder and KABOOM! This was not something to play with but the puppeteers loved blowing the mean ole Witch sky high twice a day and three times on Saturday. The more gun powder one set, the bigger the bang. The downside was the consequences for our unsuspecting audience. Not only were their eardrums now ringing, but the theatre would temporarily fill with smoke and the stage would momentarily be obscured! It was always a prank to us but when it happened, Tom would race back afterwards and raise the roof.

Interestingly his most important concern was it was artistically offensive and an insult to the opera and Humperdinck, the composer. He never got the joke – to him it was just bad taste, vulgar, a betrayal of our status as artists of the Kungsholm. His sage presence did tend to make us aware we were indeed more than a bunch of guys pushing puppets. I believe the phrase was used to poke fun at ourselves.

Once Tom made his pronouncement about *My Fair Lady* and Luis agreed, they had to go to the front office to see what could be done about it. Luis hated any confrontation in the office but not Tom. In his opinion the administration had begun their betrayal of the Kungsholm with their first decision to begin cutting operas from the rep and replacing them with Broadway fare. Tom conceded the new policy brought in audiences, but he still grouched our theater was not a Broadway house. And if we were going to present the American musical theatre then management could at least adjust their budget to support a first class production. He wanted a brand new *My Fair Lady*. While Luis nodded in agreement, Tom argued until he got the green light.

When I came into the Green Room the next day, they gave me the good news, told me to inventory the wood in the shop, and to estimate how much lumber would be needed to build a new set. I took a deep breath and replied it was no point in doing that until I had designed the set. Then I would know how much material would be needed. And so hence a new roller coaster was leaving and the climb to new heights was beginning. I was in the front car and there would be no way to avoid the terror once it reached the summit and plunged down the other side. But hey, in those days I loved roller coasters. I was, after all, only twenty-five and still more or less sailing my boat under a flag of invincibility. The extent of my willingness to get on board with absolutely no thought of whether or not I would get off without injuries can be seen in the few photos of me at work in the scene shop during that time. Tom took these shots and many more and whenever I look at them I am astonished to discern the complexity involved in the undertaking.

My Fair Lady was the second production I designed at the Kungsholm in the three years I was there. I was still unconsciously absorbing and analyzing the environment, its personalities, and searching for my particular place within it and the finished *My Fair Lady* represented the boundaries which I had yet to discover. Its design also laid bare I had not yet developed a sufficient self-editing process. Every idea that materialized in my head I thought worthy to materialize on our stage.

Luis brought me back down to earth as he calmly explained that although my plans were wonderful, they were much, much too grandiose in terms of the tech personnel it would take to run the show. I had devised complete three dimensional houses flying in and out on a dime, side views of Covent Garden sliding in and out from the wings, park benches gliding like the swans on the lake, and more staircases disappearing into the dim London streetscape! He was right. We would have needed more people above stage than below and if we reduced by more than two the understage crew, who would operate the puppets?

At first I resisted his push into my department but could at once see he was correct and so I went back to the drawing board. He challenged me to produce the same opulent concept but one needing fewer levers, wires, and rollers and therefore less people. Whether or not he was aware he was forcing me to consider the deeper concerns of running the show rather than the realization of my own little fantasies, I'm uncertain. I do know *My Fair Lady* was a much stronger lesson in stage craft and though it was a difficult period, I was concurrently growing like Jack's beanstalk.

A certain degree of responsibility towards the rest of the cast was now beginning to take hold. I began to take into consideration that although gigantic or complex set pieces looked great onstage, sooner or later almost all of them had to be

Gary with the just finished by unpainted flying houses for
My Fair Lady. 1968.

moved and usually in the dark. By that time I'd had enough experience to know the pain of a heavy piece of scenery on my fingers or toes, and the struggle to get the damn thing into its right position before the lights came back up. Tom hated long blackouts for scenery changes and their annoying influence on the audience. He even had me to sit in the booth with him to witness the uneasy vibe in the auditorium during one such change.

Understage, there never seemed enough time to complete the task. While out front, any blackout long enough for one's eyes to penetrate the dark and discern shadows moving onstage was too long to the point of being intolerable. I had to create stuff that could move easily and weightlessly but still pack the punch of the mightiest boxer. Here is where some practical knowledge of wood working techniques would have come in handy. Often I would complete pieces that would be much heavier than they needed to be if I only had the know-how to do it with less. This I would learn over time and with closer inspection of some of the early sets crafted by the master carpenters employed at the Kungsholm in the 40's and 50's.

Looking back I have travelled the road of the autodidact again and again. A waste of precious time? Most of the action in *My Fair Lady* takes place in the library of Professor Higgins and early on I decided it would be a stationery set piece and all of the other scenes would have to fly in from above or slide in from the wings. After looking at pages and pages of library books on English manor houses I decided this library should be mahogany paneled with ornate moulding and huge sliding doors. My research took me into the fantasy but real world of English architecture and design. Reproducing it in miniature, while at the same time making it light enough to be easily moved but strong enough to survive the rough handling I knew it would be get, was the roller coaster I was riding hands free.

Henry Higgins' library was a pushover compared to the struggle that would confront me in solving the problems hidden in my grand scheme of flying town houses in front of which Freddie would sing "On The Street Where You Live" to Liza Doolittle. If I had known Luis was going to give me the part of Freddie and I would be the one to negotiate my way down a set of stairs from Higgins' front door, perhaps I would have deleted the stairs. When I completed the third town house and Tom saw them, the first question he asked was, "They look pretty heavy. Do we have chain strong enough to fly them?"

I knew they were heavy, I could see it as they evolved but it was as if they had already determined their design and I just couldn't stop myself from doing their bidding.

The scene takes place at night, so of course I had rigged lights in some of the windows to boot. This added an electrical problem to what was already a problem. So I erred on the weight issue in this particular scene but they sure as hell were fantastic once their kinks had been resolved. The biggest of which was a soft and accurate landing when they were flown in. Accurate in this case meant bull's-eye. The reason was my stairs at the front door. If the stairs did not align perfectly with the center track, the puppets could not be set behind the door before its entrance. Everyone knew the solution but it was dangerous. For safety reasons, whenever a heavy piece of scenery was being flown in, that area of the stage had to be clear of people. As there were only puppets onstage, this normally was not

Gary with the unpaint library setting for
My Fair Lady. 1968.

a problem. But in this instance, the only way to locate the steps perfectly with the center track was for someone to receive the set as it descended and gently maneuver it into place before signaling the fly operator to land it silently on the stage. The puppet could then be placed. All of this had to happen in a quick black out. No one wanted to stand under those beautiful but heavy townhouses. And since I had designed the darn things, it fell to me to risk my life every night to make it all happen. This meant I would have to give up the part of Freddie to someone else.

Freddie was my first substantial role and I did not want to lose it. It was my debut in a solo number. I had practiced it to the point of doing finger exercises while singing the song to myself. But easy come. Right. The part was given to Donald with the stipulation I would get to perform it later in the run after the house threat proved itself benign. Which of course it did. The house flew in, I placed it dead center, set the puppet and returned understage, always melancholy to see my puppet working without me.

In the middle of the second week Luis told me he was switching me and Donald for the last days of the show. This was unexpected and immediately threw me into anxiety laced with dread. Donald was a very good puppet artist, not anywhere near as great as his twin, Lee, but he had a technique born out of his already three years at the theatre and worked with, if not grace, but with confidence. At this point I had been there about seven months and all of my time understage had been spent in the chorus. Although I resented it, realistically I knew I was in no way ready to take center stage. Hence all of my rehearsing and practicing.

But what had really slowed me down understage was my activity in the scene shop. Often times Luis would ask me how the construction was progressing, come up stairs to take a look and then tell me continue in the shop and he would assign someone to take my part in the show. So while my scenery work was flourishing, my manipulation skills were suffering. One simply had to be understage as much as possible to see and to absorb what was happening. Practice was fine but I had to observe and isolate a gesture or combination before I could practice it.

Before I left the Kungsholm I would solve this problem whenever I was building a new show. I simply refused to sacrifice my time understage to the scene shop and if that meant I'd have to stay until three in the morning to keep the shop activity on schedule, well so be it. The fact was, however, I had come to love being alone late at night with the ghosts and the spirit of the old mansion. But at the moment, Luis was smiling at me and telling me I'd be on with Freddie in a few days and I definitely wasn't ready for Freddie. The show must go on and so I crammed in as many solitary rehearsals as possible and literally dreamt poor Freddie.

My big night arrived and as the show progressed towards my big solo, I found myself suspended in a bubble, almost as if I weren't there. Blackout. Everybody knew this was my big night and so all eyes were on me. Scene change and the lights came up on Freddie standing lovesick outside the townhouse where Liza is residing with the Professor. The familiar opening bars of the music spilled out of the understage speakers and their counterparts were shaking the crystal ornaments in the auditorium. I launched into the song with the assurance of a kid slurping a popsicle and then froze. Just like a popsicle, I froze! Elemental stage fright had taken over without warning and I couldn't move a muscle. I was as shocked as anyone but Luis came to my rescue and gently took the puppet out of my hands, finishing the serenade before anyone consciously registered what had happened.

I was devastated and humiliated. Meanwhile proceedings continued right along and I had responsibilities with chorus puppets racing towards me in the next scene. There was no time for remorse and I quickly recovered, pushing myself to get back into the flow. When the curtain finally came down and after first the puppets and then the puppet artists took their bows, I felt like escaping the stage door before anyone could comment. That was, however, out of the question for we still had to strike the stage and put the puppets away for the night. This ritual hour labor took place at the conclusion of every show – even after the matinees. Everything had to be struck and put away.

To my surprise no one teased me or made any snide comments. Just the opposite. Everyone shrugged it off and said it had happened before and on occasion, in the long distant past, even to themselves. It was no big deal and I was bid not to fret about it and reminded tomorrow afternoon Freddie would be there waiting for me.

Years later, this incident floated through my mind with the explanation as to why it was taken so lightly. Unless the performance is done openly, meaning the puppet artist is in full view of the audience, those out front haven't a clue who is operating which character. At the Kungsholm, the only thing one saw until curtain call was the puppets. It was a No-No even for one of our fingers to be seen above stage. We were totally and utterly obliterated. No names were printed in the programs to tell who was playing which role. When we took our curtain call at the end of the show, it merely acknowledged to the audience that human hands had indeed articulated the miracle they had just witnessed. Consequently no puppeteer had any reputation beyond our understage realm. Our faceless performance relieved the pressure for recognition that normally reigns backstage in every theater in the world. So what if you screwed up. Only six people knew about it and the energy of public embarrassment was nullified. When we bowed at evening's end, we were all stars to the audience, regardless if we had played a principal or struggled with the wretched half-working chorus puppets. A queer theatre in more than one way. When *My Fair Lady* ended the standard two week run, everyone knew it had been successful and it went almost immediately back onstage about three months later. The next run Luis gave Freddie to me again without the slightest hesitation. I was more than ready for him this time.

7

LIFE OUTSIDE of the puppet theatre was also beginning to be less stressful as I came to regard the curious stares of some of my neighbors in a more positive light. After all, into their lily white space they suddenly had a young black man coming and going at all hours, in and out of the shop next door to their neighborhood dry cleaners. With no sign to tell them what kind of shop I was running, they probably thought they had reason to be concerned. What the heck was he doing in there? It didn't take long for a few of them to catch me at my door and ask me directly.

Two such people were young women around my age who roomed together in a small apartment on Clark Street about a half block away. I remember them not for any particular reason except they were art students enrolled at the school of the Art Institute of Chicago. We hit it off immediately and they in turn introduced me to Lisa. Lisa was the first hippie I had ever met. She was my age and lived alone in a studio apartment just off Clark. She was a tiny strawberry blonde with a short pixie haircut and blue eyes. She was of Polish descent and talked a lot about her right wing intolerant family. Her fantasy revenge on them would have been to take me to meet them in their home on the far northwest side of Chicago. Needless to say, I laughed with her but I had no intention of participating in her plan to bring her parents into the new world of the sixties. Yes, free love was in the air and everybody was swinging love beads but this was 1966 and Mayor Daley had just finished bashing heads at the Democratic national Convention.

I had grown up in Chicago and I knew full well where the invisible walls were erected. I may have successfully climbed over a wall at the Kungsholm on North Michigan Avenue but that was quite different than strolling arm in arm with the daughter of a Polish American immigrant on the northwest side. No way.

Lisa called me chicken and continued to tease me about the situation but she never made too big a deal about it and we happily continued our light affair. She was impressed and loved the fact I worked at the Kunsholm and she often came to see a performance as my guest. What I loved about her was her absolutely unconditional interest in the work I was doing in my studio away from the theatre. This was my first real studio and I was indeed going wild filling up the space with my paintings. I'm amazed I somehow found time to paint when I spent so many hours understage or in the scene shop. To Lisa, my real work was what was going on in my studio. And to this day I still have a painting from that period which I associate with her. She was present while I was working on it - lying on her stomach eleven feet above me in my sleeping loft (a 4'x8' piece of plywood on 2'x4's) looking down at me on the floor with the canvas. Suddenly she said, "I see a man." I responded the picture was abstract and there was no man in the frame. She asked me to climb up the ladder and look down from her perspective. And yes, there was a man sprawled across the entire surface! The colors were burnt umber and cobalt blue except for an eight inch square of bare white canvas which I had masked in tape and into which I would later write a line of my poetry or place a photograph. The man was only visible if rotated once to the left from its original position. I liked it so much that I raced down, turned it and refined the image which had magically emerged through Lisa's eyes. It's hanging directly across from me as I write these words! I have refused offers to sell it and highly treasure it to this very day.

When I moved to the North Side of Chicago, I unintentionally lost many of my friends on the South Side. These two regions of the city are worlds apart racially, economically, and culturally. The South Side, which had many black neighborhoods, is where I was raised. The North Side, which had almost exclusively and exclusive white neighborhoods, is where I grew up. Most of my friends were not coming across the Chicago River to visit me. They were completely confounded by or outright against my decision to move north and although they wished me well, they weren't following me into this unknown territory. One who had no qualms about riding the subway under the river was my soulmate Bonita Byrd.

Bonnie and I had met three years earlier when we worked on staff together with a pilot job training program aimed at high school inner city dropouts. The program was called JOBS Project and was administered by the YMCA of Chicago with federal funding. Bonnie and I were hired as counselors for the kids. It was assumed communication would be easy since we were in the same age bracket. It was a false assumption and as I look back, condescending and dangerous. Witness me getting cracked with a fist across my right jaw when one of the kids in my group responded to my words with uncontrolled anger. Bonnie and I left the Project around the same time. She got a position with an airline while I had landed my dream job at the Kungsholm after my short stint with the ad agency.

Bonita Byrd would prove herself again and again a significant person in my life and today remains one of oldest and closest friends. The office where she worked was downtown and often when she finished, she would not head home to Hyde Park but instead would come north to hang with me. Usually we would have dinner at Wing Yee, our favorite Chinese restaurant on Clark Street. Occasionally she would stay afterwards and watch me paint and when it was time for her to leave, it was the custom I would ride the bus or subway with her back downtown where she would get the IC train back to the South Side and I would get back on the Broadway bus which ran northward along Clark Street. We have acted out similar rituals throughout our entire friendship. Both always concerned we keep things as balanced as possible. Bonita would be there time and again for significant events in my life and was with me when I created my first puppet about eight years later.

The most bizarre aspect of our long relationship, however, centers on the fact she was absent for the first ten years of my Blackstreet U.S.A. Puppet Theatre in Chicago. She was there just as things started rolling and then destiny removed her and I was on my own for the next decade. I no longer regard this as either strange or with regret. The things that emerged in our lives in those years apart could not been achieved had we been together.

When she came back into my life after her absence of ten long years, it was almost as if she had never been gone.

I remember picking her from her downtown hotel to bring her to my studio for the remainder of her stay in Los Angeles. It was near dinner time and so I took her to a Japanese restaurant. Not coincidentally we had spent lots of time at a Japanese spot in Chicago the two or three years before our friendship detoured.

We began the conversation almost immediately addressing the pink elephant sitting at the table with us. Whatever had caused the rift in the first place? We batted the blame back and forth for a while until simultaneously we realized we were beating the proverbial dead horse and started the long task of catching up on what each had been doing in the decade past.

Bonita was the first person with whom I staggered through the agonizing process known as coming out. Except with her, there wasn't any pain involved. Although the beginning of our relationship had included sex, that aspect diminished in ratio to my slow acceptance I was also attracted to men. I was so far back in the closet, I had to either come out to someone or suffocate. The fear, anger, and denial was beginning to paralyze me. Her calm acceptance set me on the road to eventual peace with the whole issue. At that time I didn't understand I could not separate the components of my identity and remain at peace. Dissociation is not the solution; rather it is a delusion and a trap. The self-condemnation was criminal to myself. The scars of this battle period are still visible. Witness my consideration now to exclude any mention whatsoever of this part of my life. Of what could I possibly still be afraid?

8

THE GUYS who ran the show backstage at the Kungsholm were indeed a considerable gathering of clashing personalities. We differed in age, race, sexuality, politics, and level of education. These differences were the bottom line of all the heated arguments, discussions, and intrigues that, in a sense, were nearly as dramatic as the repertoire presented on stage. If one wanted to eat lunch or dinner in peace, our Green Room was not the place to do it. The hysterical scenarios which unfolded at that table were as unpredictable as they were either outlandish or boring.

Looking back I see that my slow adjustment to all of this was, to great measure, a defense of being in such unfamiliar territory. It took me at least a year to understand much of what seemed serious or threatening was nothing of the sort. Theatre people are a species unto themselves insofar as loving and caring for their own. But this, I think, is something learned behind the footlights through experience.

When I would take my tray off into the wings and settle with a book away from everyone else, I was actually retarding my theatrical education. And in particular, hampering the time it would take me to learn the intricacies of one of the most rarified houses on the Chicago theatre scene. As I've said, most of the people there on my arrival had been there at least three or four years. What they had to share could not be imparted in any other theater in the city. Nor for that matter, in the entire country. When I walked into the Kungsholm I walked into an extraordinarily unique theatrical history of over thirty years in the U.S.

Intermission at the original theater on
the fourth floor of the McCormick mansion. 1940's.

There was nothing even close to its grandiosity in any American city. One would have to go to Europe to the Salzburg Marionette Theatre to find an entity with a comparable aristocratic history of artistic accomplishment and longevity or to the Bunraku of Japan. These were the high royals of world puppetry arts in which the tradition is narrowed to an institution. Of course many countries have some tradition of puppetry which is part of their rich cultural heritage – for instance, the grand shadow puppet theatre of Indonesia and the antique familiar Punch & Judy. These exist, however, in a more fluid state and are practiced on varying levels of professionalism, individually and collectively. It has not been often an ornate building like the Kungsholm has been erected from the ground up to house diminutive 12 inch tall actors, and vocalists.

So here thriving and carrying on and carrying out all the necessary tasks was this wild card group of guys with absolutely nothing in common except two things. Number one and most obviously, we were all deliriously enchanted with the Kungsholm – the puppets, the repertoire, the 210 seat red velvet doll house theater with its crystal chandelier and crimson curtain, the sets and costumes, and of course the lights which, in a regular theater, can be a nuisance glare assaulting your face, but it never touched us until our curtain call at evening's end. The prestige of identifying ourselves to new acquaintances was also a plus. In short we were a tiny elite dancing about in a fantasy environment. Great. On that we all agreed.

The number two common cause was, however, something which, when awakened, could ignite bad tempers that would linger for days and days. We all voted we were grossly underpaid and under appreciated by the management.

Like theatre artists all over the world, money was not the reason that drew us to the theatre. Most of us would have been there regardless of the size of our paychecks. To put it simply, all of us were infected with virulent cases of the red and gold disease. We were dedicated to discharging our duties without any boundaries. Whatever we needed to do to make that magic happen when the curtain parted, we did. Our paltry paychecks never remotely entered into the equation. And then suddenly that all changed. Suddenly everybody was talking about it and complaining. Mysteriously we simultaneously came to the conclusion we were more than common laborers who punched a clock in and punched out.

The conversation began. How could we rectify the situation and receive fair compensation for our unique talents? Perhaps if our theater were part of the organized theatrical apparatus of the city, things would have been different. Most likely we would have been members of AGVA, the American Guild of Variety Artists, but that wasn't the case.

From its inception, the Kungsholm had been privately founded and funded by one man. Somewhere back in history he had made deals which exempted his theater from the rules that normally regulated the professional stages of Chicago. He had even managed to circumnavigate IATSE, the local stage hands union! Whatever the deal, it was still in operation some thirty-five years later and even continued to survive the transfer of ownership when Frederick Chramer died and the theater was handed over to the highest corporate bidder.

The new owners were announced to be the national restaurant chain of Fred Harvey. In the 1940's, 50's and 60's, the Fred Harvey chain was a giant corporate restaurant with a considerable presence across the States – especially on its highways. Their bland, all-American menu of meat and potatoes could not have been more at odds from the old world European high-brow profile of the Kungsholm with its elegant Scandinavian smorgasbord and expensive wines. Most likely they acquired the Kungsholm as a silver platter atop their fare of flapjacks and scrambled eggs. One of the opinions I heard constantly, inside and outside of the theater, blamed the hick brass than ran Fred Harvey Corporation for the slow demise of the puppet opera. What did Fred Harvey know about running a place on exclusive North Michigan Avenue? They were blamed for the increasingly poor quality of the food in the dining rooms as well as the reduction of our opera repertoire and the introduction of Broadway musicals into our seasons.

There was, of course, some truth to all of this and in hindsight I can understand all of it. With the advent of television and the opening of the Lyric Opera of Chicago, something as delicate, fragile and rare as the Miniature Grand Opera was destined for extinction. The Fred Harvey administrative decision to transform our classical repertoire with the injection of Broadway musicals was an admirable strategy to keep the lights on and the doors open as long as possible. Sadly it proved only a temporarily successful effort. But miraculously, just enough time for me to romp amid its dying embers and occasional flare ups for three years before everything went dark, the doors shuttered and for the first time in untold years, no ghost light was left center stage overnight.

The downward spiral of the food quality, however, was inexcusable and most likely resulted from corporate chef replacement in the kitchen. One of the new chefs had been transferred from a Fred Harvey on the Ohio turnpike where he had been flipping burgers for five years. He was delighted to be in Chicago, but imagine this guy suddenly faced with special orders from the tables upstairs overlooking one of the most affluent boulevards in the country.

But OK. So we knew we couldn't do anything about the changing repertoire or the food but the idea we were not being paid much more than the doorman seemed to grow daily in the Green Room, understage, in the locker room, in the lighting booth, and in the scene shop. There was, as yet, no plan of action to make the situation more tolerable but the steam was beginning to rattle the lid on the pot. Everybody was unhappy.

And then I suggested I could write a letter.

Needless to say, I didn't have the slightest idea of what might be on the other side of the door I had just volunteered to open. I just wanted to do something to change the vibe that was beginning to make our usual happy-go-lucky atmosphere rather unpleasant. I hadn't thought anything through but I knew something had to be done and soon.

My suggestion, of course, turned everyone's head towards me and questions began flying in my direction:

What would be said in the letter?

> Who would I address it to?
> Should we request an immediate raise in our salaries?
> How much should we ask for?
> How much do you think we can get?
> What if the response is a flat out 'No'? Strike?
> Should we write it independently of Luis who, although part of our tribe, was technically part of management in his role as director of the theater?

Of course it occurred to no one to seek out knowledgeable advice. The oldest and most experienced among us, Tom in the lighting booth, would have been the person to ask. Calling a union didn't even cross our minds. We were so isolated from the larger theatrical scene in Chicago, we really didn't see ourselves as the same breed of the actors, dancers, musicians, designers, and craft people populating backstage Windy City stages. We were pretty much on our own. And very muddled about how to proceed. We bounced the subject back and forth until it was time to set the stage for the evening performance, at which we all rather gladly launched into the work with which we felt much more comfortable. After the show and the stage was struck, everyone left the theater abruptly without any mention of the heated conversation that had taken place earlier.

The next afternoon, of course, we found ourselves sitting in the Green Room with a big pink grinning elephant. Someone finally asked what the plan was and when it was going to be launched. "Well, Gary said he would write a letter." And again all faces swiveled to me. The entire rocket was launched again and boomeranged around the room until it mutually decided Gary would indeed

Audience members standing in front of the schedule. A close reading of it reveals the upcoming productions: *Cavalleria Rusticana, Pagliacci, Die Walkure, Madama Butterfly, Faust, Il Travatore, La Traviata*. Frederick Chramers is listed at the bottom as director. 1940s.

write a letter and it would be given to Mr. Madsen, the head honcho in his plush office adjacent to the main lobby with its luxurious carved baroque staircase. As soon as I completed the task I would read it to everyone, we would all sign it and cross our fingers.

Immediately my mind began racing with regret. What had possessed me to put forth such an outlandish idea in the first place? If Mr. Madsen asked whose idea had initiated the letter and who had written it, would I tell the truth and bear the consequences? Would I lose this dream job before I learned everything it had to teach me? Was I crazy? How could I author a convincing letter echoing our belief the guys running the Miniature Grand Opera were unique not only in Chicago but in the whole world and therefore deserved the compensation we were asking? If it came to facing management across a bargaining table, would I be able to do that? And how had I become spokesperson in the first place? My big mouth.

I think it took about a week of writing and rewriting before I showed up in the Green Room with something like a final draft. I began by talking about the eminent position of the Puppet Opera on Chicago's cultural landscape, its blue ribbon history, and one of a kind profile. All this was linked with the fine reputation of our restaurant and the joy our customers seem to feel as they left their tables and paraded down the grand staircase towards our theater. From here I moved into a description of the many unseen complex backstage tasks which the theatre staff discharged so smoothly and brought smiles to everyone's faces as they spilled out onto North Michigan Avenue when the curtain went down.

My request for more equitable compensation cited the fact our salaries had not been increased in three years, the cost of living factor, and the dedication to the theatre working long past midnight after everyone else had left the building on repertory change nights. I made no demands or threats and requested management's very kind and fair consideration on the matter. Everyone was present and everyone signed it, including Tom and Luis. I bravely put it into the envelope I had already addressed to Mr. Madsen and then, as swiftly as possible, ran through the kitchen and up the backstairs, through the lower dining room, past the bar, and the grand foyer to his office. It was my first time there and as I gave the letter to the secretary, she asked what it was about. I haven't the slightest idea of my reply as my goal was to finish the dreaded task and get the hell out of there and back to the theater where I felt safe.

Mr. Madsen rarely came over to the theater unless he was escorting special guests to their seats or perhaps bringing people backstage and asking us to give them a tour. He was a tall handsome Swede with dark hair quickly receding. Very polite and aristocratic, but friendly and always impeccably dressed in a tailored navy blue suit and deep red tie. A crisp hand kerchief in his breast pocket. On those days when I arrived for work and passed through the main lobby, it was not unusual to glimpse his striking figure so different from the only other bona fide Swede in the building – Mr. Jensen, a flirtatious mousy little man who acted as host, checked reservations, and assigned theater seats. We never knew his first name but we always had to go to him to get comp seats for our friends. I was always at a loss as to how to respond to his covertly lascivious comments to me and usually sought to avoid him whenever I could.

When the matinee was over, Mr. Madsen suddenly appeared backstage. For a moment everyone froze but we quickly relaxed when, after a general hello, he asked Luis to come up to his office as soon as he was free. He then made another inclusive remark that as the afternoon audience collected their coats in the lobby, he overheard many wonderful words praising our performance. This was the first time any sort of recognition came to the theatre staff about their work. Everyone exchanged puzzled glances as he left the theater.

Luis didn't rush away but worked at his normal pace alongside everyone as we struck the set, Tom switched off the spots, and the ghost light was set in the middle of the stage until it would be removed when we reset everything at seven for the eight o'clock show.

About an hour later I was up on the fourth floor in the scene shop when Luis came up to say the first thing about which Mr. Madsen had queried was who had written the letter. Luis replied the entire theatre staff had contributed to the contents of the letter but that I was the author. That wasn't exactly true but Luis was attempting to deflect some of the forthcoming anger from me. Well intended but unnecessary as no anger materialized. Madsen commented the communication was well written and he would respond to our concerns after due deliberations. And that was the end of the meeting.

Meanwhile the Green Room was alive with anxiety, the excitement born of a new sense of power, and plain ol' fear. Our collective pride in standing up was alternately blown up and deflated. None of us had ever been involved in an act of revolution on any level and certainly not one which affirmed our status as a select group of artists. Artists who had chosen to engage their higher ups in a forced conversation aimed at their acknowledgement of the truth with a few extra dollars in our paychecks.

Whatever we had done, it wasn't as important as those brave souls who had recently confronted Mayor Daley's brute force at the Democratic National Convention or what was about to happen at the Stonewall Inn. In all of their fine colorful silks and lace, the puppets standing all around us seemed to stare in silent support and agreement. Now all we could do was wait.

The answer came much more quickly than expected. All in all it took a little over a week. Probably time during which Mr. Madsen had to discuss the situation with the Fred Harvey Corporation folk. The secretary came backstage and delivered the message. Mr. Madsen would like to see Luis after the matinee. Yikes! This is it!

As we finished our lunch and went up to set the stage, very, very little was said. Usually lots of bantering would take place at this time. Last minute casting would occur with Luis's permission and some people would trade roles to relieve boredom or just to get a chance to do something different. This happened frequently even though it was risky as Luis might like what he saw in the new interpretation and rule the switch permanent for rest of the run! Of course this was precisely the goal for some people, their way of auditioning and showing Luis they could handle the part. A more infrequent trade would find someone in the performing cast switching with whomever was doing tech. This was always a last minute decision also usually ignited by someone's sense of boredom. Tech could be exciting and it could also be the seat of power; as in cutting someone's applause short by accidentally closing the curtain prematurely. It was always done in a sense of mischief and no one took having the curtain rung down on them very seriously. They could always return the favor when the rope was in their hands.

When the curtain went up that afternoon, I would bet absolutely nobody's mind was in sync with what we were doing on the stage above us. This happens frequently to performers and probably to people in all professions. It's usually fleeting, especially if the task at hand is relatively demanding, but in the world of theatre, every artist faces the temptation to switch into auto pilot. Every artist is also aware that allowing it to happen too frequently is the kiss of death before an audience. Often, but not always, they can sense when the artist is just going through the motions. Of course some artists are masters at fooling the public and this facility comes in handy when one goes onstage with the flu or a broken heart or is thinking about the possibility this performance may be his last. And that's exactly what we were thinking that afternoon.

Had we gone too far? How dare we initiate a confrontation and campaign for a more decent paycheck? We could already hear Madsen giving Luis the news we were to clear out our lockers and get the hell out. The show seemed to drag on forever and forever. I think we were doing the Broadway musical *Paint Your Wagon* that afternoon. A show I never warmed to and for which I always volunteered to do tech whenever it was scheduled.

I couldn't wait to bring down the curtain.

For the first time Luis did not participate in striking the set. After his bow, he left understage and headed immediately for Mr. Madsen's office.

Rather glumly we completed the task and retreated in silence to the Green Room. A few people went to fetch a cup of coffee and some cookies from the kitchen. When they returned, Luis was still away so we all continued to sit. Tom came down from the lighting booth and sat with us. Being the great old guy he was, he at once told everyone to relax. "The worst that can happen is they have refused our request. No one is going to be fired. The house is booked solid tonight, what can they do? Cancel it?"

"Beyond that, where would they find replacements for you guys? These puppets are unique to the world, designed especially for our slotted stage. Even an experienced puppeteer wouldn't have a clue as to how these things work. Let alone impart some passion to them in a performance."

"And come change night, what the hell would they do? You've got the sets, scenery, puppets, costumes for every show scattered and crammed helter skelter all over this place and only you know where it's all stored. Relax." Tom's pep talk brought us back to reality and indeed everyone began to loosen their emotional collars.

When Luis finally returned his first words were, "I don't believe it, no *creo*, I just don't believe it." He had a habit of sprinkling his conversation with his native Spanish. Of course we drowned out his last phrase with a chorus of, "What happened, what happened? What happened, what did he say?"

Luis smiled and sensing his power over us, teased with a long drawn out. "Welllll, welllll, I guess the bottom line is, everybody just got themselves fired … I mean a raise!"

We all glanced around the room in complete astonishment. And then the questions went flying at Luis. "How much?" "Beginning when?" "Tell us. Tell us."

Luis's response was, "Well, what did you think was going to happen? Gimme a break. We're not the kitchen staff or the reservations clerk, or the host who can be replaced in a heartbeat." And assuming a haughty air pronounced in his most eloquent backstage camp, "My dears, *you* are the esteemed puppet artists of the Kungsholm Miniature Grand Opera. Even if you are forced to perform dumb shit like *Paint Your Wagon*. You are artistes and I am your royal director, HA!"

Everybody broke into laughter and cheers and congratulations and tossed their own camp comments into the mix. "Send up to the bar for the best champagne." "Who's gonna pay for it?"

Tom sat back and smiled at us and when he spoke, we all quieted down for a moment. His comment was level and without humor as he recounted in all of his years at the Kungsholm, the guys who brought the show to the stage had never questioned their pay. It never ever seemed to cross their minds, let alone band together and actually speak up for themselves. "And for this united effort I think everybody needs to remember Gary was the one who brought this whole thing out of mere Green Room bullshitting and wrote the letter that got you some action. "

Tom's unexpected voice caught everyone off guard – including – me and momentarily we all experienced an uncomfortable feeling. The fact was, at some level I was still an outsider in this group. I was just a little too serious and I had still had not reached the point where I camped it up with them. I never called anyone Miss this or Miss that. And although I knew everybody's backstage code name, I never used them either. My name was Gary, not Elvira, as they sometimes called me in high teasing tones.

"Elvira, your new set is just too, too divine, but girl couldn't you add a wee bit more red to those roofs?" I didn't take offense at this language, as a matter of fact I enjoyed it and understood its source but it just wasn't my style at that time. Some ten years later I came to use it to great effect but always sparingly. To this day I am more prone to say "motherfucker" than "girlfriend." But beyond that, I

Puppeteers pre-setting the stage.
Note how a group of figures are mounted on one small platform.
This enabled a single puppeteer to move several puppets
across the stage. Circa 1946.

think race still had a lot to do with it. We're talking 1968 and Martin Luther King had not been too long in his grave.

Before the premiere our new production of *Porgy & Bess,* management had contacted the Chicago Urban League to gauge their opinion. I was always aware of who I was and where I was, with the end result being I was probably perceived as being a bit uptight or standoffish. Bottom line. I was carrying the banner for the race and therefore I had to prove I was … blah, blah, blah. What a burden to carry so unconsciously into such a setting.

It only took everyone a moment to recover from the serious pall that Tom had tossed into the celebration whereupon the first comment was something to bring us back to our giddiness. "Oh, I think Elvira deserves a hundred red roses." "And a tiara with diamonds." "And earrings to match." "Hooray for Elvira!"

What could I do? This was the world I had longed to join and be accepted. Naively I was surprised to find the backstage universe of theaters all over the world had more high, happy, hilarious drama than ten Broadway comedies put together. So I said, "I'd prefer emeralds and bracelets for my ankles!" Everyone cheered and again someone called for champagne from the bar. But no one, including Tom, had any money to pay for it. For dinner that night we did, however, manage to wrangle a few bottles of sparkling cider from our friends in the kitchen. The show that evening was spectacular, we painted the wagon with mischievous abandon. Something unheard of had occurred. We had been recognized as real artists by the management. Or had we?

Visitors are briefed by a technician on the stage of the original theater in the ballroom on the fourth floor of the McCormick mansion. Circa 1940s.

9

I THINK this historic backstage episode registered higher on my personal scale of self-confidence than any of my heretofore artistic achievements as a member of the puppet opera. Sure, everyone lauded my set designs and my ability to wrestle them into reality in the scene shop, but somehow my stepping forward and my willingness to be the point man in the salary scenario alerted me that I had more to offer than I'd imagined. What a surprise. I had always seen myself as shy in most social environments. I still do. It's not an unusual self-image for an artist.

Artists realistically need solitude to accomplish their work. So what had just unfolded was some kinda freak accident? Or was I really capable of standing at the front of the line and voicing an opinion everyone would respect? The whole darn thing set me off balance for quite a while until Luis came to me with his proposal for the new production he wanted to see on our stage six months hence.

In a conference with Mr. Madsen it had been decided we would follow the lovely *My Fair Lady* with something totally its prim English opposite. We would go honky-tonk, raunchy, glitter, and gauche. We would do *Gypsy*, the hit Broadway musical fashioned from the autobiography of America's most loved and best known stripper, Miss Gypsy Rose Lee. What did I think? What did I think? What did I think, indeed. No one had ever asked me what did I think about the selection of new repertory before.

Well, shit. I thought it sounded great! Luis smiled. Now all I had to do was to buy the cast album and find out what I really thought. I had no aversion to honky-tonk, raunchy, glitter, and gauche. Hell, I grew up listening to my Uncle

Cedell play his recordings of Muddy Waters over and over until I went to sleep. And I loved Halloween. I didn't yet have a gimmick but instinctively knew this entire stretch of my life was my big chance. Later I was to discover one of the hit songs in the *Gypsy* score was entitled, "You Gotta Have a Gimmick." Lots and lots of glitter and even more raunch. I was going to have a ball designing the set for this show.

So off I went to the library again. The first book I checked out was the volume Gypsy had written which had inspired the show. The other books I searched failed to deliver the inspiration I needed so I decided to scout some areas of Chicago where remnants of the landscape described in Gypsy's book might be found. Cheap hotels and small burlesque houses.

After giving it some deep thought, I realized an exact replica of what I was looking for was actually still standing at the south end of State Street roughly between Polk Street and Van Buren. As a teenager, I was very aware of this district, a grouping of small seedy theaters with marquees that actually used the word "burlesque." They could be seen when riding the A Train El just before or after it emerged from the tunnel running under the Loop, Chicago's spectacular downtown district. I vaguely knew what they were and their fascination for me stemmed not so much from the taboo but that they seemed almost haunted, like some forgotten relics from the days of Al Capone. It never entered my mind to investigate them closer, let alone attempt entry. About as close as I ever got to them was exiting the south side doors of the State Street Sears & Roebuck department store, which put the theaters about a block away. At that time the entire area of State Street south of Van Buren emanated a dark feeling. Dingy grey run down two-, three-, and four-story buildings, a few parking lots, and the theaters. The theaters that once upon a time probably glistened with the electricity of the forbidden, branded, evil entertainment of strippers. No doubt one of these theaters witnessed the triumphant performances of Miss Gypsy Rose Lee!

Rather than take the bus, and as it was a warm day, I walked there from the Kungsholm. Only a few ghosts still stood. Most of them closed, filthy, and boarded up. The marquees cracked and broken, some still holding a few sad rows of tiny clear light bulbs which had once flashed and flickered. A few had been taken over by cheap clothing stores. I walked past them and then crossed the street to get a different view as I ambled back. As I doubled back for the second time, my vision telescoped down the street and I decided to explore a bit more. Sure enough, the flea bag hotels were not far away. But unlike the theaters, they were still the same flea bags they probably always had been and – surprise! They were still open. None more than four stories. Some of the signs above their doors read simply "Hotel." Black steel fire escapes ran up the front or down the sides of them all. Clouded grey glass and tied back curtains and two to one grey sheets and bedbugs. This was the road Gypsy had trudged to become the One and Only she eventually became. I had found my inspiration, and instead of walking back down State Street, I skipped over to Michigan Avenue and followed it back north to the Kungsholm.

I went straight up to the scene shop to check what lumber was still left over from *My Fair Lady* and then sat about for a while mulling over what I had just seen on State Street and daydreaming about what my *Gypsy* would look like.

The beginning of a new set was always a rough period for me. Although this would be my third production, I still lacked confidence and felt myself an impostor. I was constantly comparing my work with the extraordinary sets built before I arrived on the scene. Of course I never reminded myself these sets were the results of a collaborative effort between several people. First, a designer who conceived and planned, and then the master carpenters who actually brought the design to three dimensional reality. I was only one person and nowhere near a master carpenter. I was flying high on the genes passed down by my grandfather who, with the help of two others, built a four bedroom house for his wife and six children in 1920. The first black family in town to have an indoor flush toilet!

I had spent every summer watching Grandad measuring, hammering, sawing and creating something magical from the heap of scrap wood stacked behind the chicken coop. Although I now recognize the valor of that history and honor it, in the Kungsholm years, my ancestors did not consciously influence me. My need to exceed the perfection I saw all around me was not altogether healthy and I would accept no excuses for myself. For indeed, what about Fosser's stuff?

William Fosser had been one of the former directors of the Kungsholm. I pieced together from around 1960 to '64. Fosser was a trained genius theatrical designer with extraordinary carpentry skills. His talent was remarkable not only in building sets but also in painting exquisite backdrops and scrims.

And he worked alone. He also had designed and created an alternate rod puppet which fit into the tracks of the Kungsholm stage. He had actually attempted to supplant the Kungsholm puppets with his own design and went so far as to create an entire production of *Kismet* in which only his puppets were used. This arrogant act cost him his job and he was replaced by David Pennington. The rogue production of *Kismet* complete with Fosser's puppets, however, remained in the repertoire. The theatre bought the whole show from him and ushered him to the door.

None of us, except Luis, was ever much good at operating the Fosser figures. They were completely unlike the Kungsholm puppets and had none of the ease and grace to which we were so accustomed. They were about two inches taller which gave them the appearance of grandeur on stage. They were also three times as heavy and were always getting stuck in a track. All of us loved *Kismet* but we hated the puppets. The fact was, Fosser had disappeared so quickly, he had not adequately trained anyone to manipulate his creations. His imprint on our theater was indelible. He had crafted a technique of forced perspective construction so convincing that a foot of space appeared as twenty feet. I examined his work over and over and over. This was the work of one man! And now here I was, the one man, running the scene shop. I had to measure up.

Now I don't remember making any preliminary sketches for I am not a sketcher. But in retro, I surmise something was put on paper before ordering lumber. I do remember I would make thousands of measurements on the replica stage I had built in the scene shop. And then, just to be absolutely sure, I would go down to the theater and check my numbers again!

Once I was sure everything was going to fit, and being very conscious of the heights my structures would reach and whether or not I'd have to build extension masking to prevent the audience from seeing into the wings, I would walk over to the lumber yard on Clark Street near Erie and make my order. I was never given any budget restrictions on how much I could spend on wood. I simply chose what was needed, told the clerk to charge it to the Kungsholm, and deliver it the next day. I always thought this interesting because almost anything, other than the lumber we said was needed for a new production, was questioned at the front office and usually required a meeting with them to explain why such and such was necessary.

Just such a brouhaha erupted when Luis decided he wanted a strobe light effect for the scene in which Mama Rose sings a gradually tempo-escalating song entitled "Have An Egg roll Mr. Goldstone." Luis' plan was to drop in the strobe just at the point when the song becomes so raucously fast and the words whiz by so quickly they can hardly be understood. The puppets would also be racing back and forth across the stage at breakneck speed. The strobe, of course, would intensify everything, making it appear like a speeded up silent movie. The office replied it was an unnecessary expenditure and the funds would not be approved. Luis contained his decorum for a moment and then allowed all of his Latin temper to affirm every stereotype in the book about Hispanic fire. After his speech about each department of the Kungsholm respecting the expertise of those in charge of their particular realm, he asked to be allowed to run the kitchen for a day. Has the chef ever been denied an extra crate of lettuce? The strobe light was ordered. And for the next week Luis stormed through the theater fuming about the backward vision of the imbeciles upstairs.

There was one other production expense, however, that was never questioned. Costume fabric. Every new adventure needed fresh material to construct the costumes for the debut show or to replace old outfits which over time had grown worn, lackluster, or simply struck our costume designer as outdated or boring – even if the designs were his. I don't know if David redesigned so many old costumes with a valid reason or if indeed he was just racking up hours on his timecard. But between the end of the afternoon matinee and the call to set the stage for eight o'clock, it was not uncommon to find him in the wardrobe room with the sewing machine blazing. David Traversa was an immigrant Brazilian and Luis' roommate. Like Luis, he spoke other languages, but unlike Luis, English gave David some difficulty. Often Luis translated backstage conversations using Spanish.

David was an aspiring women's designer and a part-time student at one of the fashion schools in downtown Chicago. He was a part-time employee backstage and very rarely came understage to operate puppets. Once in a while he would be drafted to handle a few chorus puppets for some of the big crowd scenes of the operas. But his puppet work would often draw attention to a part of the stage which should have been in the background so Luis used him understage sparingly. Nobody, while doing their big aria in the center spotlight, wanted to be upstaged by David clumsily trying to keep his characters still.

David said he loved dressing the puppets but his fingers; normally so nimble in wardrobe, turned to spaghetti when he tried to command a puppet during performances. All of us were more comfortable when during the show we could hear David's sewing machine softly buzzing in the background. During a blackout he was a dangerous wild card. He constantly zoned out when everything went dark with the inevitable result of someone crashing into him or vice versa, creating a momentary havoc while we scrambled to assess the damage and right the situation before the next light cue. As I've said, scene changes were razor accurate and had to be incredibly swift. A pileup understage would happen which resulted in a pile of puppets onstage. "Oh shit! Get those guys off the stage! David! Get the fuck outa here. We'll deal with it. Go!"

The reason, of course, there was never any complaint about fabric expense was it was nonexistent. How much yardage does one need to dress a figure no bigger than a Barbie doll? Even if David fell in love with a very expensive piece, one yard would do the trick. Beyond that, he was so inventive with the mountain of remnants in the fabric bin, he rarely went shopping. Luis always told him he didn't need to recycle but David felt if he was on a roll, he didn't want to interrupt the vibe by facing the shopping crowds and walking against the icy wind to the fabric store.

The results of his labor immediately hushed all argument. Mind you, these were Barbie doll measurements! How he switched so effortlessly from his life size work at school to these diminutive emotional creations remains a mystery. It is most unfortunate no documentation exists of his Kungsholm work. David came out of school and almost at once began to make a name for himself as one of Chicago's newest designers. His work at the Kungsholm continued until the end. Probably much owing to his friendship with Luis.

10

ONE OF THE great gifts the Kungsholm bestowed upon me continues to serve me well today. The habit of procrastination faces untold numbers of artists in every field of creative endeavor. Whether facing a blank page, an empty canvas, vacant score paper, or a room full of expectant dancers waiting to be told what to do, the artist must conquer the urge to hesitate or run. To postpone. In my case I was confronted with a vast space, void and menacing. What would I do with it? OK, so I had now completed all the homework. I had turned countless pages at the library, read the autobiography, scouted the hard pavement of Chicago's former burlesque district, listened to the score until I knew most of the songs by heart, drawn and discarded a few sketches.

A trillion unrelated questions and thoughts now crowded my head, the most insidious reminded me this was my third show and I really needed to make it a spectacular of spectaculars. I had to top what I had thus far produced. I had to prove to them I was better than they ever imagined. I had to be the wonder boy of miniature theatrical design and set construction. I had to! Needless to say, with this conversation raging in my head, there was scant room for any creative ideas to nudge their way forward. I fell into the deepest well of procrastination ever dug. And the days ticked by.

The lumber arrived. Day after day I found myself rambling through the scene shop and finally leaving with absolutely nothing accomplished. I was totally aware something was amiss but had no idea how to extricate myself from the pit. Fear had begun to nibble. The premiere had been scheduled for four months hence. A month passed – still nothing.

One afternoon after the matinee Tom came up to the shop and startled me from an intense gaze out onto Rush Street below. I'm sure he had expected to see the beginnings of what he had come to call, "Gary's little miracles." Now remember, Tom Doyle had been watching the parade at the Kunsholm from his observatory in the lighting booth for a very long time. He was in his early sixties and when he climbed all those stairs up to the shop on the fourth floor, he expected to be rewarded with new images in the viewer of his camera. He had praised my idea to build the replica of the stage and when he found it looking as though the show was over and the set struck, his face clouded over. To this day I thank him for the wisdom of his words. As his eyes swept the room and confirmed there wasn't one speck of new construction, he walked over to me and said, "You know, Fosser used to get stuck too. And your work is every bit as good as his, if not in some ways better. Have you been up to the old burlesque district on State Street?" I was shocked at his question and the depth of his assessment of what was needed made me freeze. "Well," he said, "That's a good start, I'll be back again later."

And that was it. That was all. He didn't make a speech of understanding or remind me in three months our red and gold would rise on the new production of *Gypsy*. He didn't have to. How he knew has gone with him to his grave. Thank you, Tom Doyle.

I didn't start or get anything done that afternoon. Instead I clocked out and went around the corner onto Michigan Avenue to Stuart Brent Books. Mr. Brent's shop was one of the tiny jewels of the grand shopping boulevard. An old world atmosphere crammed with idiosyncratic titles and shiny art volumes presided over by Brent in a starched white shirt and tie, and a staff of two people. I remember him as being rather handsome, short, muscular, probably in his late forties with thick salt and pepper hair. Intellectual and engagingly cheerful. During the past year I had wandered into his store often enough for him to strike up a conversation. His curiosity had bid him to delicately ask a few questions and he was delighted to find out I was one of the theatre people from the Kunsholm. Once he knew my story, he always greeted me with enthusiasm. A young black man browsing the shelves at Stuart Brent on North Michigan was still an oddity. It had become my habit to pass time there between the matinee and the evening performance. I think it was there I bought my very first copy of Kalil Gibran's, *The Prophet*.

Usually I used my time in the store turning the pages of the big expensive art books and occasionally Brent or one of his assistants would bring me a pair of white thin cotton gloves. I probably looked quite the character in that setting, dressed as I usually was in blue jeans, a T shirt and sweater in the summer or my cozy navy blue sailor pea coat in the winter. All of this was very often accented by clinging sawdust or paint specks if I had come over directly from the shop. Despite scrubbing, my fingers were alternately blue, yellow, or red if I had been painting. No wonder the cotton gloves. Mr. Brent and I exchanged a few pleasantries and I disappeared into his fantastic world of pages and more pages. Presently I sensed it was time to return to the theater, hoping there was something special in the kitchen to fuel up for the show ahead.

I didn't think much about it at the time, but rarely did anyone except Tom come up to the scene shop to see what I was doing. Well, I take that back because Charles Wilson would occasionally quietly appear while I was sanding or sawing. As the only native American Indian on the staff, Charles enriched our multi-cultural brew. He had been the first staff to greet me on the night I threw my destiny into the hands of David Pendelton when I interviewed for my job. I remember even now how very, very proper and soft spoken he was. Officially he was the host of the puppet theatre and ideally suited to the job. I was consciously aware of his grace and charm as he greeted the patrons entering the theater. He had a gimmick which immediately won people over. He would take their tickets, examine them sternly and then with a smile tell them much better seats were available and he would usher them there if they so desired. Well, of course they desired, and Charles would lead them to very choice seats which were probably the very seats they had been assigned in the first place! Three years later when I had summoned up enough courage to make my first visit to Chicago's only gay bath house, I was bowled over to find Charles behind the admittance window assigning lockers. Although he exclaimed when he saw me, he was too busy and I was too embarrassed to stick around and make conversation long enough to find out if he was allotting choice lockers to the prettiest boys.

Like David Traversa, Charles also was occasionally drafted to push puppets when we needed an extra pair of hands. And like David, Charles was equally if not more uncomfortable and klutzy in this capacity. But at the Kungsholm, everybody pitched in, regardless of their reservations when Luis decided they were needed. And so as soon as he had seated the last person, reluctantly but dutifully Charles would snatch off his red tux, black tie and appear at the last minute understage and ask for his directions. He was always given chorus work and, as he knew the repertoire backward and forward from his usual place at the back of the house, Luis was confident in giving him very brief notes.

But still everybody braced themselves. Charles tended to be very careful and attentive to the puppet in his hands. He was so focused, he would inevitably neglect one of the crucial skills of understage navigation. Steady balance and control of the four wheeled stools on which we all sat and on which we whirled and propelled ourselves in an unbelievable choreography throughout the performance. If one lost authority of the stool, one usually ended up with a crash – feet in the air and butt on the hard floor! The music in the theater would, of course, completely mask the sound of the catastrophe but the puppet would be left temporarily deserted, hopefully just rocking about and not sprawled on the stage like its operator understage. This accident could happen to anyone and we all had our turn meeting the cold tile. Charles took a chance every time he sat on one of our four wheeled little demons. Once a month we oiled our wheels but Charles always insisted we skip his. We did.

Wilson's other niche at the theatre was either taking over the lighting booth completely in Tom's absence or working in tandem with him when the lighting plot Luis designed called for Tom to have four hands. The booth was probably state of the art when the theater was built but by the sixties, it was a little behind the times. There had to be at least one hundred lighting instruments, plus ten border lights, footlights and ancillary special instruments hanging above and in front of our stage. The circuits, dials, and levers to control all of this made the front of the booth look like the cockpit of Flash Gordon's rocket ship. The booth was located just above the last two rows in the balcony and commanded an excellent view of the stage.

Once or twice I sat up there with Tom or Charles and found myself hypnotized by the complicated ballet they had to perform on cue to run the show smoothly. The dimmer dials were the size of dinner plates and usually demanded when one was being swiveled clockwise, another one, sometimes a great stretch away, had to simultaneously be twisted counter-clockwise. I realized they had to listen to the score as attentively as we did because many of the cues were a mere two or three bars of music and sometimes just the silence which followed as a violin disappeared into the ether. One could not nervously anticipate, but had to sit in calm awareness until the moment arrived. The Joker in the deck was the unpredictability of the movements of the puppets. Everything onstage had, of course, been choreographed, blocked, and set, but often mishaps understage might delay the arrival or departure of a puppet. This happened just enough so the lighting booth had to stay in high alert to catch and cover the mistake as it unfolded. Luis was fairly indulgent, however, in allowing us some leeway of creative movement when one commanded the stage in solo performance.

The arc follow-spot was usually used during such intervals which unleashed us to explore the set inspirationally. We had the freedom to wander wherever we desired, as long as we returned on time to the appointed place where other characters were scheduled to meet us and made sure we were out of range of flying or rolling scenery which might be activated during a blackout. There were enough backstage stories of unfortunate puppets who had been led by their unthinking puppeteer into a zone where they looked up or sideways to see a house or two bearing down upon them without time for escape. No one wanted to be the guilty of what we jokingly called "puppetcide."

There was a big box bulging with puppet spare parts in one of the prop rooms – a graveyard of arms, legs, heads, rods, springs, ball bearings and wire skeletons. Although useful and fruitful when an active performer needed surgical repair, it reminded us the box existed basically because of our human negligence.

Tom and, to a lesser degree, Charles were both masters in their realm at the top of the theater. I don't think any of us understage recognized how crucial their contribution was once the curtain went up. They were aware there was an Electrician's Union in all Chicago theaters except the Kungsholm. The union regrettably had decided to switch off the light on them.

As I think back on Charles' occasional appearance in the wood shop, what I remember most is our shared awe and appreciation of what the scene artists of the forties and fifties had accomplished in the pinnacle glory of long past years. Our opera repertoire had been gutted as management loaded the scale heavier and heavier in favor of Broadway and many of the opulent set pieces of the operas had been moved up to the shop where they now sat covered in layers of sawdust. The magnificence of some of these pieces still echo for me.

In particular Charles and I admired and marveled over the miniature frescoed ceiling of Scarpia's chamber in Puccinni's *Tosca*. This is the ceiling under which one of opera's most spectacular and honorable murders unfolds and whoever designed and executed the scaled-down baroque scenes meant for this work to mirror and amplify the music and the moment. It resembled the Sistine Chapel in precise minutia – angels, and great busted virgins, saints and demons, nude muscular men with stern faces all floating in a backdrop of billowy clouds and gilt gold curlicue. This was the last glorious fragment of the original *Tosca* set and represented the Kungsholm at the heat of its cultural fire. It weighed a ton which is probably why it had survived for so long. Charles, like Tom and myself, was very much wrapped up in the history and mystery of the Kungsholm. But all that remained to tell the story pre-Tom were these startling beautiful artifacts of theatre romance crystallized into wood and paint. Their elegance and perfection testified in a voice as matchless as it was silently fading. None of the other guys, including Luis, seemed to care much about these things. They sort of took it for granted to work surrounded by all of the affluent craftsmanship and rare artistic expression.

The historic photographs of the Kungsholm in this book I found on a shelf in the woodshop under ancient cans of dried up paint, dirt, and sawdust. I squirreled them away and never showed them to anyone. Several months before I had uncovered a color photo 8 x 10 of the interior of the theatre. It had been shot at a very strict angle which showed off all of the grandeur of the room. The closed crimson curtain, the frescoed ceiling with the huge chandelier, the red velvet seats and the private boxes on each side. When I brought it to the Green Room, Charles pulled rank, saying it had once probably been exhibited in the display case outside on Rush Street and he would take it to Mr. Madsen. Instinctively I knew he wanted it for himself but I withdrew from confrontation and let him have it. Damn. To me this incident again demonstrated my outsider status and that all of this European spectacle was in some way basically foreign to me. Sadly I accepted this bullshit, but at the time I had yet to realize the falsity, perpetuated by motives of unacknowledged selfishness and greed. I returned to my realm on the fourth floor.

11

THE DOMINANT form of the *Gypsy* set finally began to emerge as a fantasy rendering of one of the flophouse, run-down hotels in the burlesque district of South State Street. I was building a little piece of sorcery featuring disappearing walls, transformative windows and doors, and lots and lots of fire escapes racing in every direction that bound the whole edifice together. It stretched across the entire stage and was planned for a upstage position to allow drops and glittery curtains to descend in front of it when needed.

Once I launched into the actual physical act of measuring and cutting wood, I knew I was safely off into the project's orbit and could trust its gravitational field would keep me on course until all the energy was spent. This meant I usually transformed into a man with a one track mind for the duration. As the work progressed, the set would gradually mutate into a structure sometimes slightly different than the original vision. This tended to manifest in the form of embellishment more than any serious change in the design. It was not unusual to create and spend unreasonable amounts of time on details which served no authentic purpose other than fulfill my need to prove I could indeed produce something so intricate. It was also not unusual for me to remove all of this extra baggage as I neared what I thought was the point of completion. The whole process was a constant building up and tearing down.

Tom and Charles declared I was a madman with a hammer when they discovered something I had spent the last three days constructing would suddenly disappear on the fourth. In actuality, I had to make concrete some of my ideas before I could decide if they had any valid impact. How did the placement of such and such alter the scene of which it would be an integral part? Was I merely making something pretty? Who ever heard of a pretty flophouse? This is not an elegant townhouse on the Eastside of the park in NYC. It's a should-be-demolished crumbling pile at the wrong end of State Street in the Windy City. I was challenged to fight my tendency towards elegance and cute again and again.

This was never more clear than in my concept for the train station scene where Rose and her gang sing the song, "Together." I told Luis I was building a red caboose into which all of the characters would disappear as the locomotive departed with the lights dimming to a purple sky and big orange moon This could prove to be a problem but I assured Luis I would build the thing low enough so none of the puppets would encounter difficulties in boarding. With our technology operating from below the stage, it was a near impossibility for a puppet to rise from the surface more than four inches without the fingers of the puppeteer becoming visible. Needless to say, fingers onstage was a serious offense and would set Luis into a serious lecture on the basics of controlling the figure one was operating hitched with our responsibility to maintain the illusion at all costs.

Against this background I confidently jumped into designing and constructing my little red caboose. The caboose, of necessity, multiplied into three railway cars. The first two cars had to be positioned as if they were disappearing into the wings to allow for the tech person to invisibly pull them off with the caboose attached at the end. This idea came to me in the middle of working on the main set piece, the hotel. I delayed the caboose and passenger cars until the very last minute. The last minute meant just that – Change Night, the night before the opening at the matinee the next day. Change Nights into existing repertory was difficult in itself but changing into a brand new show made everybody exceedingly nervous and explosive. There simply was not enough time to accomplish everything needing to be done before two o'clock the next afternoon. Nevertheless we did it.

Actually I didn't bring the caboose down from the workshop until the next day, somewhere around ten in the morning. Everybody was busy with a thousand tasks – weighting the flying scenery, rehanging the drops we had hung the night before, writing out the tech sheet, last minute lighting adjustments, and fussing with the new cast of puppets. The rehearsal would begin at eleven. There would be a short break for everybody to rush off to the kitchen then converge in the Green Room where Luis would give last ditch notes on what had occurred during the run-through and then … "Shit. It's two and Tom is bringing down the house lights."

Joining in the fray, I sat the caboose down in its appointed spot over the 6th track. Everybody turned and immediately there was a flurry of "Oh how cute," and "Elvira, girl you've done it again!" I connected it to the other two cars and pulled the train off two or three times to make sure it would move as effortless as I hoped. It did, hooray. The next thing was to check its accessibility for the three puppets who had to board it. I called Luis, Lee, and Roy and asked them to get their puppets to test it out. They had no trouble stepping up the two small steps and disappearing into the cabin. As a matter of fact, it proved so easy, Luis decided he wanted the train to slowly chug out of the station as the three characters ran for the caboose and jumped on while it was moving! Ultimately this proved problematic and the stage action was reduced to the only one puppet making the run and jumping on board. Luis would not trust this stunt to anyone on the first day and after a few runs, he developed a spectacular run and jump that was wonderful to watch. Everybody was thrilled with the little red caboose and this great piece of acrobatic action it had inspired.

In the middle of this, Tom came down from the lighting booth and called Luis to a conference out in the third row. He then asked me to reset the caboose over its place on the 6th track and then yelled up to the light booth, asking Charles to turn on the spots for the train scene. They both took a deep slow look and then Luis said aloud, "You're right, it's off, it looks like a toy." At first it didn't register to me exactly what they were talking about. The rest of the crew had finished their tasks and wandered off to the Green Room. Tom yelled up to Charles again and asked him to bring in the red and blue border lights to see if that would make a difference. Now I understood the focus of their activity was my caboose. I felt myself immediately tense as I asked what was up. Luis asked me to come out into the house where Tom began to explain there was a problem with the caboose. Flatly stated, from the audience it appeared as though a child's toy had been set onstage.

This no-nonsense critic of my cherished prop produced a cramp which shot hot throughout my body. Up to this point I had been kind of the wonder boy who could do no wrong in the scene shop. And now they were negatively evaluating something which had given me a great deal of pleasure while creating. Luis seconded Tom's opinion and then Charles called down from the booth to ask if he should try another lighting combination.

 As the punch to my fragile ego slowly subsided, I sat down in the row just ahead of Tom and Luis and did my best to look at the thing objectively. Luis asked what I was thinking and commented further the thing looked too brand new. This was supposed to be the last car in a train that had been crisscrossing the filthy railroad tracks of the nation for God knows how many years over miles and miles. Since when has anyone seen a caboose with gilt gold handrails? Meanwhile Charles took it upon himself to try a few more lighting tricks until Luis told him enough. This was a problem the lights could not camouflage.

A long silence passed until somewhere inside me the more sensible Gary Jones took control and admitted yes, I had missed the train. Tom's next question was whether or not I could fix it before the evening curtain, due to rise in about four hours. Now although the more sensible Gary had seen and agreed indeed something had to be done, Tom's urgent request was too much. The thought suddenly overwhelmed me that I would actually have to completely alter if not destroy something which had emerged from one of my creative revelries. And I rebelled. I said I would try to fix it but first I had to consider which route to take and what exactly needed to be done. Luis responded it was simple, "Just tie a rope to it and drag it up and down the alley across the street for a while. It just needs aging Gary." I cringed as I rose from my place in the second row, climbed up onto the railing of the orchestra pit, and leaped in a short cut to the stage. This was a no-no for the simple reason there had been times when guys did not leap wide enough and their big feet landed in the orchestra resulting in damages to our puppet musicians and their tiny instruments. Luis said nothing about my transgression as I picked up the caboose remerged into the theater stage right and up the aisle out through the foyer.

Now this was not the route to go during business hours. I knew perfectly well one did not go walking through our elegant lobby carrying a prop from the theatre. But I was hurt and pissed. Pissed at myself for succumbing to my penchant to make pretty things and hurt, unrealistically, because my comrades had pointed out the error. As I walked through the lobby I encountered a few patrons who had obviously gone into the bar after the show and were now just leaving. When they noticed me and my caboose, one remarked, "Oh look there's the cute little red caboose, isn't it just too divine. I'd like one just like it for little Jack's birthday." I smiled within and at that moment knew for certain I had strayed way off the path.

When I got up to the shop I decided the best way to age something is to break it and then repair it haphazardly. I went back to the stairs which led up to the fourth floor, set the caboose down, and with my foot wished it bon voyage. With lots of noise it tumbled over and somersaulted to the third floor landing with a big loud crash! Our bookkeeper, whose name I can't recall, had her office a few feet from where it came to rest and she came running with an alarmed look on her face. As she surveyed the scene she said, "Oh Gary, and after all of your hard work, and it was so cute. "

Needless to say this, another confirmation of my cute demon, pissed me off even further. I picked up the pieces, I had destroyed the gold railings, and broken two of the wheels, I told her not to worry about it. I also knew the damn thing still needed more serious realignment but shoving it down the stairs again was not among my options. Instead I headed back up to the shop with it. I sat it and the pieces on one of the plywood workstations supported by very old saw horses and contemplated the next move. Soon I seized one of the tools I had never used before, a wood chisel, and began to gouge random channels and paths in every direction across the surface. I then whacked it a few times with a hammer. Amazingly the thing had not completely disintegrated under the abuse but when I finally paused momentarily from my violent creative spasms, I sensed I was on the right track. I reattached and glued part of the railing and remounted the wheels which were now kinda lopsided and pounded in a bunch of nails randomly where they served no purpose further than effect. The last thing was a new paint job and wash over its entirety. I mixed a couple of shades of rust, brown, and gray and applied them without reason, layering, and overlapping boundaries. Finally I streaked my masterpiece with energetic arcs of black using a very worn paintbrush. Voila! The whole process of rebirth had taken about two hours. It was now a little after six as I left it on the table, aimed one of the big floor fans at it, and hurried down to the kitchen to grab something for my rattled stomach before the eight o'clock show.

Neither Luis nor Tom was in the Green Room when I got there and all conversation stopped for a moment when I sat down. Finally someone asked, "Well, are we gonna have a little red caboose tonight?" I was not to be amused and my answer was something on the order of, "Surprises are best at the very last minute."

The whole episode demonstrated once again how fragile my feelings were in this place. I could never really let my guard down even though these guys would have been the last to inflict any intentional harm. Their experience of black people was so limited as to be embarrassing but they were not in the least troubled by it. They liked me well enough and certainly respected me, but it never crossed their minds to censor a casual remark easily interpreted as racist. Big black dick comments were common. What so bothered me about this little interlude? Looking at it some thirty-five years later, I can see I had gradually come to occupy a unique place in the hierarchy backstage. Especially after engineering the stupendous pay raises everyone was enjoying because of my accidental leadership role in writing the letter. Indeed I realized that's why Luis had asked my opinion when he first broached the subject of doing *Gypsy*. Lately my opinion about a lot of things was asked where this had never been the case before. I understand now it was this new special unspoken rank I enjoyed and wanted to keep. The drama of the little red caboose threatened this and revealed I had feet of clay like everyone else. What I didn't comprehend at the time was the plain fact I really didn't have to do anything extra to fulfill my specialness to them. The mere fact my black butt was there at all made me unusual in their eyes. No doubt this same scenario was being acted out all over the country as black citizens nationally began to move through the many doors which had been so long closed to them. Unfortunately we were all treading these unfamiliar trails grappling in the dark completely alone.

Soon enough everyone was finished eating, Tom wandered in with his usual cup of black coffee, with Luis following a few minutes later. Luis lived within walking distance of the theater and often went home to eat with David in the evenings. Bottom line, he hated the spiceless food of Scandinavia and couldn't stand the thought there would be no peppers left in the pot when he got home after the show. Neither he nor Tom said a word about the caboose. When time came to go up to set the stage I journeyed up to the fourth floor to see if the fan had done its job. It was still wet in some spots but well … what the hell. I'd read many a theatrical account of scenery going onstage dripping. I picked it up and made my way to the theater, the back way through the kitchen. When I came out to the stage right wing, I sat it down on the 6th track and hitched it to the other two cars. No one said a word, but everyone was looking. Luis at once asked for the lights for the railroad station scene. As a matter of fact Tom had switched them on before Luis began his request! Luis and I went out front and a few of the other crew followed.

A few adjustments in beam intensity were made and the effect was startling. The difference was so apparent and so right, Charles blurted out from the balcony, "Now we're talking! That's great." The little red caboose had disappeared into a cocoon and now spread its wings a brand new being. I told everyone to be careful, that it was still slightly wet in a few places. My comment didn't produce any reaction, everyone was smiling and soon melted into their pre-show responsibilities of setting, positioning, checking, and tightening. The curtain was lowered and would go back up in less than an hour.

The caboose drama capsulized the entire road leading up to the completion of the *Gypsy* set. I had encountered a few other challenges on that road but they had surfaced at the beginning or middle of construction and I'd had time to address them. For a while the dag-gone fire escapes gave me the devil. They kept looking like stairs instead of fire escapes and it took me more than a moment to relinquish my first designs – cast aside what had already been produced and start all over. The reason they looked like stairs was because I was building stairs. Each little step was a solid piece of wood instead of the five or six strips of rod iron typical to most escapes. Once I realized my mistake, I groaned at the thought of the work involved in doing it right and almost abandoned the motif. But I knew they would be beautiful if I handled them correctly, and besides, what would the ghost scene builders of the Kungsholm past think about my skimping on design to avoid a little extra work? I buckled down and got to into the hard, rewarding labor. I had a tradition to uphold. And certainly I could never let it be said the quality and inspiration in production dipped with the arrival of the first black scenic artist, could I?

The black cross of my ancestors seemed to forever drag me down and supply the energy to rise ever higher and higher. Their demands were sometimes outrageous but always, in the end, proved a point and a prophecy. All of us really are of the same star stuff and the oppressions of the past I need not allow to impact the dreams and efforts of my present reality. Mysteriously the fiction that some of us were more royal than others would no doubt continue to enthrall and blind untold unfortunates. And the powers at the top would continue to manipulate the lie to a degree so sharp as to make it appear true. That my awareness of this great centuries old drama for power and wealth was connected to the temporarily derailing of my creativity as a young artist is testament to the benefit of knowledge. Even though unnumbered and invisible forces surrounded me with a resounding "No you can't." The blood of past generations which knew the truth flowed thick enough through my veins to force me to keep going towards the "Yes you can." And I'm talking about my white blood as well as the black, if one wants to be specific.

I ended up cutting hundreds of pieces wire about three inches each which I glued to my wood stair frame, four 3-inch segments per step. It was a monotonous task but when the entire structures were sprayed black and gray with a hint of rust, I had fire escapes any inspector from the fire department would approve! I hung them like Christmas tree ornaments all over the hotel which produced a sense of imminent danger and decay. These were the avenues of exit the inhabitants would use to escape their dreary lives within. Never mind the avenues were themselves rusted and rotted and were probably more risky than the disaster within.

Interesting that I had realized the need to age the exterior of the hotel and had consequently intentionally broken and mangled the fire escapes at the same time I had scarred and aged the walls but had not applied this logic to my beloved caboose. I guess its cuteness just overwhelmed me.

12

THE DRAMA of the caboose was not, however, the only catastrophe that overtook us on the opening of *Gypsy*. One of the central scenes of the show is the spectacular metamorphosis of the skinny teen into her new self as the greatest stripper in the business. It's cannily accomplished with the memorable song "Let Me Entertain You" as sung by Sandra Church in the original Broadway production. The beats and words of the song accent item after item of her costume being cast to the stage floor until she is almost bare, but never quite, before the blackout.

The logistics of getting the puppet to strip was a nightmare even for our resident genius David Traversa. It was finally decided to pin the costume with straight pins to which would be attached thin lengths of clear fishline. When the music indicated a piece of the ensemble be removed, someone would pull the line attached to the pin and hopefully gravity would take over. During rehearsal it was revealed this plan was rife with possibilities of fingers appearing onstage but there was no other way. The two people cast were neither happy nor confident. As our reigning diva puppeteer, Lee George usually waltzed into these new prima roles eager to imprint it with his flamboyant and matchless manipulation technique. This was the second time he would have to synchronize his movements with a partner since the *Porgy & Bess* rape scene trauma and I could tell he was not about to take the blame if something went wrong. His fingers would not be seen onstage, on that you could bet.

Luis allowed him to choose his best understage sister, Roy Slocum, to pull the pins. For the first time I saw David Lee rehearsing between the matinee and evening. Luis gave them access to the sound board and our ears rang with the rhythms of that damn song every day until the show opened. The occasion gave everyone something to tease David about. "Girl, since when have you had trouble getting out of your clothes? We know you don't even wear panties."

Roy, of course, tried to boost morale and constantly reassured David they would be OK once the show got rolling. "Maybe opening night might not glide but eventually all of the bugs would be shaken out. Mark my word, this is your Aunty Em speaking and I know what I'm talking about."

It wasn't funny.

By the time the hands of the clock spoke eight o'clock sharp and Charles had seated the last guests, no one was smiling backstage, understage, or onstage. The matinee had been uneventful and although the song had gone smoothly with all of the pins and costume falling nearly on cue, there was no pizzazz or sizzle to a number which everyone knew had to sear and fry or die. We knew David could do it and we were rooting for him but thus far it had not happened. The afternoon had also belched up the crisis with the damn caboose and now it was about to be pushed semi dry out to the wolves of Tom and Charles up in the lighting booth.

Nothing was amusing. Shit. House lights down, chandelier dimmed, spot on the conductor's entrance, his bow, I raised his baton, Luis pushed the button on the sound board and the tape reels began to spin. Curtain up, we're off.

The caboose no longer looked like a toy and as it chugged off stage left I breathed the relieved air of victory. There were no other moments of critical concern except the moment of semi-nudity which still lay ahead. The soundtrack boomed in the voice that by now was all too familiar, "Ladies and gentlemen straight from Wichita, presenting Miss Gypsy Rose Lee!"

The big, big number unfolded in the single laser beam spot light surrounded by darkness. It followed a trajectory of rising expectations starting off teasingly slow and steadily rising towards the finale as piece after piece of the costume was stripped away. The slow start was good as it allowed Lee and Roy to feel the audience and gauge their complex choreographic challenge accordingly. But as the temperature began its upwards, unstoppable spiral, the legendary fabled accident occurred. Every creative regardless of discipline, photography, painting, music, dance, or acting can recount one of these famous storied accidents. The act of chance that suddenly blossomed, usually in reaction to a previous mistake or attempt to prevent a calamity, a last ditch effort, some rash and outrageous move by the artist that said, "What the hell! What can I lose now? I'm gonna do this, like so, and toss my chips into the air. Like it or not, here goes."

The third pin got stuck and the garment did not fall. The cue passed and the deadline for the next layer to come off was approaching like a rocket. The huge tape recorder spun the reels and the music sailed on. Roy tugged at the fishline, and to everyone's dismay, resulted in a freaky hopeless tangle between the line before and the one about to be pulled. Would that cue gallop by too? No fingers could go onstage. Were there any press in the opening night audience?

And then it happened. Out of shear desperation and smack on the beat as though it had been meticulously planned and rehearsed, Lee gave the puppet two little jumps and two of his understage famous trills or shimmys as we called them. The effect she had danced out of her clothes was unbelievable! Up until that moment Lee and Roy, guarding against just such a predicament as the one in which they now found themselves, had concentrated on holding the puppet statue still while the pins were removed. And now in a flash of crouching, puppet movement history had been extemporaneously created which eventually became a high mark of the show. Needless to say, Lee repeated it every night although the pin and fishline rarely got stuck anymore.

In art, the contest that raged between years of practice, training, and planning on the one hand versus the incredible grace-filled accident on the other, had tonight clearly illuminated the glorious mysteries of chance. Shades of Cunningham!

When the curtain came down, everyone climbed from understage with a big grin. Tom and Charles came back with a few people for the usual special guest tour. We were cordial to them but to each other no one said much about what had happened beyond, "Wow, that was close." I think we were all waiting for the next day to see how Lee would exploit and embellish or ignore what had transpired. It is not unusual for an artist to attempt to dictate his will to the muse. And what had happened had not been Lee's will. Some other force had slipped in and upstaged him. He had temporarily lost control. The puppet had taken the reins and ushered him and everyone else into some alien zone. Just who, indeed, was really running the show?

I've been on this particular treadmill myself from the first minutes I began to perceive myself as an artist. The questions are at once a celebration of something larger than oneself while at the same time smothering and deflating the ego of specialness which lurks, longing for recognition in even the most insignificant creative act.

Protecting myself from the battering encountered by the average American artist while simultaneously surrendering to what, for me, has become a proven truth is the balancing act I confront daily. Giving credit to the unknown, when one's audience is unaware the unknown had any hand in the unfoldment, is a hard thing to do. I would like to think most artists acknowledge the mystery privately even though they cannot resist taking the credit publicly. It will never be known what percentage of the art hanging in museums internationally came into being through an accident. And further up the road, how many paintings were intended to be one thing but gradually, during the birth process, detoured from the artist's vision and became something else?

Artists frequently discuss the phenomenon of a work taking on a life of its own with openness and candor. They talk of going with the flow rather than risk being devoured in resistance. In my experience, to struggle and fight paves the way for doom, confusion, and failure. Back then, it all just seemed like several miracles had saved our butts and the reputation of the puppet opera. The miracles were incorporated into the show and we settled in to enjoy, as best we could, the last days of our new show. The kitchen staff had taken to good natured catcalls for us to take it all off when we passed through their domain. *Gypsy* had indeed been a great choice to add to our rep.

13

ONE WOULD think with all of the effort, hard work, long hours and outgoing energy I was expending at the Kungsholm, I would have had scant creative juice for the challenge of my own little storefront studio/ gallery up on Saint James Place. The space had necessarily transformed itself into a gallery for the simple reason the hard evidence of my art activities were beginning to crowd my live/workspace at the back of the store while the front was completely bare except for my bicycle and four chrome and leather director's chairs I had purchased to dress it up. How I found the time to work at home, in the midst of all the frantic activity at the theater, is still a mystery. There was, however, definitely some mystical relationship between my two creative kingdoms.

Generally if a lot was happening at the Kungsholm, that energy followed me home to my studio where it continued to dance and fling ideas in every imaginable direction. Amazingly, even though I spent much less time at home, new work was constantly materializing. Some days I would clock twelve hours or more at the theater, board the bus home, and then dive directly into a painting on my floor. I guess in lots of ways I was still in my superbro mode, or like many artists, I simply operated in a perpetual gear of driven activity. Everything had a sense of urgency. Nothing could wait. It all had to be done NOW, if not yesterday. With the Vietnam draft working its magical disappearance circus daily, tomorrow was not considered.

I was an authentic theatre kid, blindly enamoured, and fevered by the red and gold disease. A kid who had stumbled onto the fantasies of the life of an artist in Paris or New York through stories and books fed to me by a neighbor when I was still a teenager. These were the tales I used to vindicate living in a cold storefront with scant heat and no hot water, shower, kitchen or bath. I was living on the Left Bank or down in the Village and I traded my drawings for a meal at the delicatessen down the street.

All of this romance and art history lore had come to me from a neighbor. Minnette Lall was a young, recent college graduate who rented a room from Mrs. Morphis. Remember Dorothy Morphis was the woman who first introduced me to the Kungsholm. Mrs. Morphis taught 6th grade at the local Chicago Public School in Altgeld Gardens (now famous as the site where President Obama began his career as a community organizer). She and Minnette had met in college and when Minnette was assigned the same school to begin her teaching career, it followed they decided to share expenses. With four kids, Mrs. Morphis needed the help and the arrangement allowed Minnette to ease herself from home and into a place to begin her new adult life. At sixteen I was briefly the boyfriend of one of the Morphis fifteen year old twin girls.

Minnette was a young African American woman of penetrating intelligence, beauty, and sense of adventure. She was exotic and unusual. Her father was from India and her mother hailed from Trinidad. Minnette had a collection of Edith Piaf records long before the name had any recognition by American audiences. She would play these records for me and talk about bistros on the Seine and bull fights in Barcelona. I was mesmerized. She spoke about Kafka and existentialism and read Jean Genet. Her interaction with me assumed I was travelling on a parallel course even though she knew half of what she discussed was beyond me. She talked anyway.

After a year of teaching in Altgeld Gardens, she applied for and received an appointment as an elementary school instructor on a military base in France near Paris. To celebrate, Minnette decided to throw a bon voyage party. The contract was for two years. She was overjoyed. Vividly I remember her idea to decorate the basement of her parents' house as a Parisian nightclub. Red and white checked tablecloths and candles perched atop empty Chianti bottles in straw baskets. Of course Lautrec posters had to adorn the walls. And inasmuch as her budget nixed buying them, she commissioned my girlfriend, Diane, and me to create them from scratch.

Minnette recognized both of us were budding young artists and this was another way she conveyed to us her opinion and confidence. We launched into the assignment with a vengeance in our studios. A corner in the basement at Diane's house and a corner in the basement of mine. These were little areas each of us had commandeered for our solitary separate artistic pursuits. That Minnette referred to them as our studios produced a magical feeling of importance and purpose heretofore off our radars.

When I think of the immeasurable positive influence Minnette had leveraged so lovingly and unintentionally on my future, I am overcome with gratitude. Diane and I met our deadline to deliver our creations onto the dining room table a couple of days before the big night. Both of us had been very secretive about our designs. Minnette had taken us to the art supply store and purchased big poster boards, two apiece for each of us. When the work was laid on the table, the room was crowded with people – Mrs. Morphis, the twins, their younger brother and sister, Minnette, and myself. Diane was the first to unveil her's. She had drawn in pencil and then painted in tempera bold letters over illustrated dancing figures. She had an extraordinary aptitude for drawing and everything was rendered with precision and detail. Color carefully applied. Nothing overlapped. Everybody went "Ahh," and "Ohh" while she basked in their approval and praise.

What I had produced could not have been in greater contrast if purposefully planned. I had created two three-dimensional surfaces using strips of torn paper and glue picturing the Eiffel Tower and the Arc de Triomph. The lettering was unregulated and painted directly onto the board. For me it was an experimental process which had engrossed my full attention. But next to Diane's, my stuff looked like a sloppy kindergarten. Minnette and Mrs. Morphis responded with praise and for the first time I heard the word collage used to refer to a work of art.

This was also the initial experience in which I registered a conscious fear of being compared to another artist and their work. I was aware I could not draw as well as Diane but something inside me yet confirmed I had something else to offer beyond a perfectly rendered face or hand. Minnette and Mrs, Morphis intuited this and downplayed the rivalry. The posters were auctioned off at the party and Diane and I received a few bucks for our devotion.

Shortly thereafter, Minnette boarded a plane at O'Hare airport to begin her two year adventure abroad. And soon letters began to arrive with fancy French stamps. Even while away, she continued her campaign to broaden my experience and make me aware of the wide world beyond the South Side of Chicago.

She sprinkled her prose with the new language she was learning and described life in the fabled romantic country. Soon she was urging me to go the bookstores near the University of Chicago in Hyde Park and ferret out the poetry of Valery and Appolinaire. And of course I had to read Camus. She talked of her visits to the fatally beautiful museums, palaces, and theaters, and of seeing all of the great French masters and the classic masterpieces. Through no fault of their own, none of this inspiration could have come to me through my hardworking parents who were, nevertheless, keeping a roof over my dreamer's head.

By the time Minnette returned, I had graduated from high school and started college. My room was decorated with prints of Lautrec, and Miro and I had a prized collection of three Piaf albums which I played only when my parents were out. In short time I had dropped out of school, landed my first full time job, and moved away from home. Not surprisingly it was Minnette who made the connection for me to sign the lease on my first apartment in a building in which she had close contacts. It was from this first apartment three years later that I had moved to the North Side of Chicago seeking my life as an artist where Chicago's artists were reputed to live, work and play around. That I had so far succeeded and that my life resembled so much my learned ideas of what a young artist's life should be, I attribute solely to Minnette.

At some point during my second year at the Kungsholm I had acquired a medium sized model band saw for my home/studio. In the scene shop there were two large professional band saws which had become my favorite tools. Once I had familiarized myself with their capabilities and used them to create things unimaginable, I had rattled on so much about them that one of the few friends I had, who actually had credit, allowed me to purchase a saw on his Sears account. I am forever indebted to him and his faith in my talent.

Sherman Carter was one of the very few young black men who had chosen to live on the Near North Side. I cannot emphasize enough how rare it was to find people of color actually living Near North in those years. He shared a three bedroom townhouse with two other guys and had allowed me to temporarily crash for a couple of months at his place until I found the storefront on St. James. I count him, along with Minnette, with whom he had attended high school, among the younger angels who supported me in my first steps towards my artist identity. He was a psychologist who supervised a vocational ed. program at the downtown headquarters of the Jewish Federation of America. He'd spent time in

Russia and lots of other exotic places. Although a bit of a snob, he was nevertheless a role model who devoted some of his time to encouraging me.

The addition of this piece of equipment to my home shop literally set it ablaze. If I wasn't working on the band saw at work, I was working on the band saw at home. Its buzz, buzz, buzz rang in my head twenty four hours. It not only made tasks like building painting stretchers far easier but induced all kinds of projects I never would have attempted without it.

Significant among these was my immersion in the designing and building of chess pieces. The game of chess had always fascinated me because it was indelibly attached to my childhood. On my mother's side of the family, my grandfather and uncles spent hours in silent combative meditation staring at a chessboard. I would stand statue still and watch. Occasionally I'd ask a question but even if I got an answer, it never penetrated or transformed any of the sheer gothic silence shrouding the game. I learned how to play but the last time I sat in front of a board, my opponent fried me in three moves!

It was probably in the window of one of the North Michigan Avenue chic shops where I took notice of a very unorthodox chess set. Although recognizable to anyone who played the game, the carved pieces in this set strayed far from the usual shapes common to most boards. I believe what hooked me was my amazement each piece was a miniature piece of sculpture. Shortly thereafter, I found myself at the lumberyard where I purchased a few small pieces of pine with which to experiment.

My love affair with my band saw was about to get even more intense! The life I was now living in my tiny under-heated storefront was the imagined creation of what my existence would have been had I actually moved abroad. Although still in the same city as my family, I was existing in a world so different, it actually seemed like a foreign country. I was most often the only dark face in the crowd and the language and voices I now heard everyday were new and often vaguely hostile to my presence.

After Minnette's return from France, I thoroughly ingested and digested every scene, word, and description she shared. As it was obvious I was not going to get my passport anytime soon, I had unconsciously chosen this alternative and risky road in Chicago. Landing the job at the Kungsholm cinched the fantasy with its daily dosage of crystal chandeliers and red velvet. I was in a world not geographically far but still, very, very far from the South Side neighborhood of Chicago

Kungsholm Theatre in Miniature
PRESENTED BY
KUNGSHOLM SCANDINAVIAN RESTAURANT
100 EAST ONTARIO, CHICAGO, ILLINOIS 60611

MUSICALS IN MINIATURE, II

Selections from

THE SOUND OF MUSIC

(Rodgers and Hammerstein)

SCENE: *Austria in the 1930's*

CHARACTERS

Maria	Mary Martin
The Abbess	Patricia Neway
Rolf	Brian Davies
Liesl	Lauri Peters
Captain von Trapp	Theodore Bikel

    Maria, a novice, finds it difficult to adapt herself to convent life and the Abbess suggests that she go out in the world and take a position as governess. She is sent to the home of a retired naval officer, Captain von Trapp, a widower with several children, and soon finds that she has fallen in love with him. When she learns that he is to be married to the Baroness Shroeder she wishes to return to the convent but the Abbess and the children persuade her to remain at her post. Captain von Trapp and the baroness soon realize they are not meant for each other and their engagement is broken. The captain then discovers that it is Maria whom he loves and she agrees to become his wife and be a mother to his children.

MUSICAL NUMBERS

1. I Go to the Hills .... Maria
2. How Do You Solve the Problem of Maria? .... Nuns
3. My Favorite Things .... Abbess and Maria
4. Do-Re-Mi .... Maria and Children
5. You Are Sixteen .... Rolf and Liesl
6. The Lonely Goatherd .... Maria and Children
7. Edelweiss .... Captain, Maria and Children
8. Climb Every Mountain .... Abbess
9. Finale .... Ensemble

Production designed and executed by the staff
Staged by Luis Tacoronte
Costumes designed and executed by Roy Slocum and David Traversa
Music preparation by David George

INTERMISSION

CONTINUED ON BACK PAGE

where I grew up. The home turf was only an hour subway and bus trip away. So how had I wandered into another universe?

With opera arias or Broadway show tunes ringing in my ears, I would arrive home, typically around midnight, and dive straight to the center of my own work. The acquisition of the bandsaw created an unusual sort of mystical relationship between my two work spaces. There had been an unstated but very definite line. The dominant media at the Kungsholm was wood, while at home I was definitely focused in paint. There was some minimal crossover but now, all of a sudden, both places smelled the same. Just how and to what measure my two creative identities fed and inspired each other continued to fascinate and confound me for years. I lived knee deep in sawdust and paint in one and worked submerged in paint and sawdust in the other. Neither was a jealous lover. And I did not feel torn.

Once I had decided to design and produce a chess set to rival what I'd seen on Michigan Avenue, it was if some untamed chess spirit suddenly took control. My home shop became laser focused in a storm of opulent creativity aimed at this one goal. It lasted for the next two years wherein I made sixteen different sets. I designed a total of one hundred twenty-eight pieces and made patterns for each. Individually I cut, shaped, sanded, and painted five hundred and twelve little pieces of wood! The largest were the three inch tall kings. The other pieces descended in size down to the pawns. I recognize now I was working in miniature at both shops.

I built pedestals and exhibited them along with my paintings in the front of the store which by this point had begun to look and feel like an honest-to-goodness gallery. Its public inaccessibility, however, continued to frustrate people. But I was at the Kungsholm all day while continuing to work late into each night. I would often find notes under the door asking me to post gallery hours. But the only hours I could have realistically opened were mornings between 9 am and 12 noon before I left for the theatre. My night owl work habits made this next to impossible. If someone actually gained entrance, it was on a Monday when the theatre was dark and I miraculously heard them rapping on the glass door over the buzz of the bandsaw.

Although work with the chess pieces was hypnotic and fulfilling, I was still drawn primarily to painting. Painting, after all, was my mythic idea of what an artist does with his time. That my activities at the theatre and my emerging interest in sculpture as represented by the chess project also identified me as an artist never entered my mind. Ridiculous. But that was the narrowness of my focus at the time. For me, to be an artist meant to paint oversize canvases of mysterious content sans all narrative and romanticism but brimming with irony and revenge, high energy and anger.

Oh! And of course one had to freeze in an under-heated studio. The sixties of course were in full swing but I had come of age, if not awareness, moulded by what I knew of the artists of the Beat era. When my beat sensibility collided with the Black Arts Movement I found myself suddenly challenged by the color of my skin. Was I black enough to be a black artist? In retrospect, the question is laughable but even today, in the 21st century, there is still an annual show in NYC devoted to displaying, selling, and promoting Black Art recruited nationally.

Consequently two of the painting series beginning to dominate every canvas I stretched, were my responses to the unanswered query. How black are you? Are you a panther or a card carrying life member of the NAACP? When are you going to visit the mother land? And most important – when are you going to grow an Afro?

Combined, the two collections spanned about four years, yielded several sales and finally culminated in a one man show at Chicago's famous black cultural haven, The Southside Community Art Center.

So I was quite the busy bee during these times: a mind boggling schedule of paintings, and carvings, unbelievably interwoven with ten to twelve hour daily sprees at the Miniature Grand Opera. I was in a hurricane of beatnik operatic fertility. And yet to smoke my first joint. Amazingly things were about to get even more complicated.

14

A NEW production had just been suggested by the front office and for the second time Luis had come to me to get my opinion. Over the last year or so he had gradually but increasingly scouted my thoughts on a thousand things going on understage. Naturally his behavior was imitated by the rest of the cast and the process was so subtle, no one thought anything at all had changed. But indeed, a shift had occurred with everyone's consent, conscious or unconscious, and as it centered on me, my awareness slowly began to urge closer attention. No notice seemed taken when someone cracked I would be the next director if Luis should ever make good on one of his threats to quit if we didn't shape up. It had become a sort of joke to ask "Miss Elvira, Assistant Director." Except for one sour face, everyone laughed.

Eventually, after emerging from a mild disbelief, I pin-pointed everybody's change of attitude towards me to the pay raise I had won for us and in which they had cast me as their hero. This one act coupled with my position as the production & set designer had set me into an authoritative niche completely uninvited.

Historically all money issues and production design responsibilities had been filled by whomever was the director of the theatre – the last two being William Fosser and David Pennington. Luis, although very much in charge, had never been officially named director, regardless of the reality, it was he who kept everything running smoothly. When Pennington was let go, Luis just naturally stepped into the void to avert a collapse. Whether or not he met with the front office, affirmed the title, and asked fair compensation, I do not know. His rule derived principally from his musical authority, linguistic skills, and probably seniority. None, of course, had been there as long as Tom who, though devoted to the place, was completely uninterested in riding herd over a bunch of puppet pushers as he sometimes called us.

Lee George, our prima donna, had most likely been around as long as Luis but Lee was completely satisfied with his position, concerned about nothing more than his leading roles. Except for Roy, none of the others, Donald, Charles, David Traversa or Sean, could even remotely have taken charge for a day. It was Luis personally, however, who unintentionally put me in the hot seat by constantly asking my opinion about this or that. Everyone witnessed and, as stated, followed suit. Some grudgingly. Specifically Roy.

Roy appeared on the scene about a year after I began. Or perhaps I should say he reappeared. He began to appear in the Green Room as we checked in an hour or so before the matinee. He knew everyone and seemed very comfortable and at home understage. He was casually introduced to me and the bantering and dishing continued with the usual jocularity, hyping everyone until it was time to set the stage and prepare for the curtain. Often he stayed for the show, sitting on an extra stool understage or sometimes standing in the wings at stage level with whoever was doing tech.

One afternoon I walked in and found he had been added to our cast. Luis assigned him parts immediately and I discovered he was conversant with the operation of the puppets. From this I deduced he had worked for the theatre in the past. He seemed to be relearning everything. This was not in itself unusual, as former puppeteers occasionally dropped in to say hello. But for me, this was the first time one such person had been hired. Before the theatre finally closed, I witnessed this phenomenon was not unheard of. People would join us, leave us, join us and then leave again. The family tradition which rules theatre culture was in vibrant operation at the Kungsholm. Once in, one would never be totally out. There was, of course, also a practical side, considering how long it took to train a new recruit. Eventually the front office put a stop to it and declared new applicants be hired.

Roy was a decent puppeteer but was completely devoid of the passion for the puppets which is essential to delivering a memorable performance. His talent, however, clearly was out of sync with his capabilities. Luis recognized this and in spite of his finagling for leading parts, Roy was given only secondary responsibilities. Interestingly Lee would sometimes campaign Luis to allow Roy to have a spin at one of his leading ladies if a matinee performance had a small audience. With nothing really at stake, Luis usually gave his nod.

Lee, although the superior artist, was buddy-buddy with Roy and obviously admired him. Not artistically but just as importantly, socially. Lee was five foot five, a mousy ordinary looking little guy. Plus he had a twin. Roy was six foot, fairly good looking, extroverted, aggressive and every week had a new story about the latest black man he had seduced! Many gay men are no different from their straight counterparts in regard to public boastful narration of their sexual conquests. Of course behind the footlights, this is the sparkling juice of Green Room entertainment and anyone willing to bare his ass usually has every corner of the space hypnotized. Roy's favorite expression in the middle of these story performances was, "The blacker the berry, the sweeter the juice," followed by a gigantic deep sly laugh.

I, of course, was horrified to hear this phrase coming from the mouth of a white boy. Needless to say, he used it to great effect, always producing a guilty group roar and a sideways glance at me. Looking back, it is painful to see to what degree race and sex were unapologetically orchestrated into the complex and fairly new phenomenon of close social interaction between blacks and whites. My presence backstage had no doubt put a damper on what was said. But only temporarily. Ironically, once I was accepted as one of the gang, things reverted to business as usual and I was expected to take it all in stride.

I don't believe Roy was intentionally targeting me or, for that matter, had any malevolent intention. His behavior grew naturally from the shameful history of white America's relationship to their fellow black citizens. Before I arrived backstage, none of the guys at the puppet opera had ever been so closely associated with a black person. That I in no way dovetailed with the blackface stereotype from which they had previously operated demanded a response outside of the box. If and when dicey issues arrived with a surprise, they were usually handled with humor. The jokes almost always diffused the embarrassment and everybody, including me, would quickly move on.

Now, of course, remember this was all taking place while Bobby Seale was gagged and chained in a Chicago courtroom not far from where we sat. And twenty minutes due west, the Black Panther Party storefront offices had been ransacked, and trashed by Mayor Daley's finest. I clearly remember riding the

The puppeteers on the set of *H.M.S. Pinafore*, 1970
l-r bottom row: Charles Wilson, Roy Slocum, Lee George, John ?
l-r top row: Steven ?, Luis Tacorante, Gary Jones

bus past Chicago Federal Savings Bank at the corner of Clark and North Avenue on the morning after its gigantic plate glass windows had been smashed by the Weathermen and other demonstrators at the '68 Democratic Convention. Police were everywhere. Although at the Kungsholm I was cocooned in a dream of gold and red velvet, there was no way I could avoid the very real chaos reigning over the city. I was aware there was something off key and perhaps even a slight danger in the air for me, a black man walking down North Michigan Avenue. Rather than feeling privileged, on my way to my prestigious job I felt anxiety in the awareness of my conspicuousness. Daley's men in blue were notably unkind to my kind. In contrast, my co-workers functioned as though the history changing scenarios sweeping the country were totally irrelevant. To them there was nothing at all to be concerned about. "The blacker the berry, the sweeter the juice."

My confusion and obvious connection to the zeitgeist was mirrored in my tendency to separate myself from the group. When everyone was in the Green Room camping and laughing it up, I would be either sitting out in the empty theatre reading or up in the wood shop making busy. I remember Luis calling out to me across the rows of vacant seats and coming over to ask if everything was OK and why wasn't I in the Green Room with everyone else? Of course I had no answer, shrugged off his concern, and in an attempt to mask, I would close the book and head to the Green Room. I would be greeted with an enthusiastic yelp of "Elvira, where have you been?" The conversation would continue and often times I would open my book and resume reading. This didn't seem to bother anybody. At least I was in the same room with them and everybody was happy.

Things never came anywhere near expressing a rivalry with Roy but I always sensed he alone was none too pleased with my position as production designer. That Luis consequently consulted me whenever a new show was considered vividly confirmed my status. Ironically, although flattered, none of it made a difference to me. It had all unfolded too smoothly, almost magically for me to claim any credit. I had miraculously been in the right place at the right time and simultaneously discovered I could pull off what it took to get the show onstage well before the deadline. The words production designer had, heretofore, been non- existent in my vocabulary. I had no ambition to run the theatre, I was simply just enjoying the heck out of this fantastic setup in which I found myself.

Roy, however, was privy to none of this and it was obvious that he had lots of ambition.

There were no other power slots in the theater which could conceivably have led to the directorship. Roy invented one. Somehow he insinuated himself into helping David Traversa create and sew the costumes and thereby became assistant wardrobe designer. David really didn't need any help and had demonstrated he could effortlessly knock out whatever was needed whenever it was needed. But during our down times between new shows, he had increasingly taken time off to devote to his newly emerging couture reputation. In David's absence we frequently found Roy in the costume shop sitting at the sewing machine. Usually he took it upon himself to repair a costume. Most often the clothing was not in an emergency state and could just as easily have been washed or sent to the dry cleaners. But after removing the garment, Roy would replace it with a new one of his own design and, in an off-hand way, declare a change might be good, what do you think? Inattentively Luis would nod and continue with whatever current task was engaging him. Slowly this pattern altered everyone's perception until one day it was no longer unusual to find Roy in the costume shop. He now had a position in the theatre beyond being just another puppeteer. Consequently he seemed to relax his attitude toward me.

15

LUIS, however, continued to keep the backstage management circle limited to himself, Tom, and me. And when he announced a new show was to be added to the repertoire, everyone in the Green Room was surprised and excited except Tom and myself. We had known about it for a couple of weeks. The latest razzle dazzle would be the legendary *The King and I* and was about to set new levels of frustration, glamour, and outrageous behavior behind the tiny footlights of our grand miniature opera house. The main chandelier would not fall but we sure as hell would dangerously rattle it. The costumes would be designed and executed by David Traversa and Roy Slocum! This was to be the show calling on resources I was unaware I possessed.

By this time I had been at the Kungsholm for about two years. I knew every dark glittering corner – both of the theater building and the adjoining McCormick mansion which housed the restaurant. Without planning any of it, I had somehow landed in this tiny yet significant jewel in Chicago's cultural landscape. I was as yet unaware of how the Kungsholm fit into the city's theatrical history but instinctively intuited its importance and by extension my responsibility to continue the legacy at the high standard I witnessed throughout the building. All of this, of course, magnified by my race oversensitivity.

I knew also I had pretty much free reign to design and build whatever my imagination conjured for the new production. This would be my fourth show and my only competition, aside from the ever present historical scenic masterpieces which constantly held up their superiority, would be my *Gypsy* which was already six or seven months old. For some reason *The King & I* was at least on my radar screen. I had seen the movie as a teenager but black faces at Broadway road shows were fairly uncommon when Mr. Brynner criss-crossed the country and almost every woman and some of the men in the audience imagined he was extending a personal invitation in the show-stopping tune "Shall We Dance." The musical score and the forbidden possibility of the on-stage interracial love affair combined with Yul Brynner's bald head had made *The King & I* a blockbuster.

It was a management decision from on high that it be our next offering. I would be willing to bet the final catastrophic series of events to overtake us a year hence had already been glimpsed by the office and their sudden interest in what went on our stage was the consequent result. Usually it was Luis and Tom who would come up with the idea for a new show and together plead for permission to go forward.

Once the King was declared our official new playmate, the familiar glow and gloom, eagerness and dread, love and fear slowly began to weave its operatic environment. The first thing always needing to be ascertained with a new production was the size of the puppet cast. Once that number was uncovered, the new puppets had to be found. As there were rarely virgin puppets waiting in the wings or sitting on the shelf, this meant Luis had to scrounge and scavenge for figures wherever he could find them.

His first stop would always be the chorus puppets of shows already up. Although this method made his job easier, it simultaneously created a headache for David and Roy who would have to undress these characters and re-costume them for the new wave and then change them again when the older show revolved back onto the stage. The fact many of the garments were literally sewn onto the puppets tripled the effort and sometimes witnessed costumes accidentally destroyed during the effort. Ideally every show should have its very own set of puppets. Impossible as there were simply not enough puppets.

So off David and Roy would go to the graveyard – the ancient bin of puppet parts. Arms, heads, legs, torsos, operating rods, springs and things that, when assembled with care, could yield a brand new puppet. David Traversa was a master at this task. He complained lots, but usually under his hands the needed figures would eventually appear. His most inventive idea was the restructuring of the ancient smashed up puppet heads. With a hot glue gun he developed an intricate technique of sculpting new faces over the derelict remnants of the old. Born of necessity, it quickly became the normative procedure. *The King & I* required about twenty children among its cast. Aside from *Porgy & Bess*, it was the only show needing kids. Luis refused to raid the kid cast of Porgy for the most obvious reason – the puppets would need a make-up change in addition to their costumes. NO!

David didn't argue and by the time rehearsals began, he had used the glue gun to create round chubby cheeks and new noses over the discards at the bottom of the graveyard bin! The march of the king's children always produced lots of giggle and whisperings in the audience.

Meanwhile I had descended on schedule into my usual dungeon to face the dragon of new production concepts. I was miserable. The deadline was three months away but at this point, my panic attack quotient had registered me not worth reviving.

Good old Tom came to the rescue and brought me his copy of the original souvenir program from the Broadway production. For atmosphere only. He allowed me to study it for about a week and then reclaimed it. From there onwards I was on my own. Tom said he wasn't worried and waved me off to the library to get lost in as many books as possible about ancient Thailand. Personally he thought the *King & I* was a great choice for our theatre, but not for the same reasons as management. Tom explained here was a royal story that fit perfectly into our tradition of miniature spectacles. What could be more outrageous and glittery than the King of Siam lounging on a golden throne among a harem of wives, attendants, children and eunuchs, towering temples, fortresses, and of course the royal palace itself! This was pure Kungsholm stuff and if I couldn't ascend and float off into these heights … well.

Needless to say, this was Tom doing what he did so well – injecting a little derring-do where required and sitting back to watch the resulting fireworks. I did not disappoint him. Although I have no photographs of my King, I do remember it as not my best set but certainly my most sumptuous, glamorous, and glittering. I began with the royal staircase. It curved and gracefully descended into the grand ballroom where "Shall We Dance" would unfold. The inspiration for it was not, however, from any of the research materials now cluttering the shop at work and the shop at home. Anyone who looked deeply would have immediately recognized its predecessor in the grand hall across the lobby from the entrance into our theater. We saw it every day and often raced first up and then down on our trips to the scene shop and back to the theatre. No one seemed to notice the

The Kungsholm Restaurant grand stairway which inspired Gary's stair set for The King and I.

similarity. Its construction proved quite a challenge and midway through I began to get glimmerings this was not going to be an easy task.

When Luis, Tom and the rest of the backstage crew saw what I was doing, they all agreed the ultimate action in the show would be the descent of Anna and the King from the top of the stairs into the ballroom. Realistically, however, there was no way this could be done. A marionette can negotiate steps but not a rod puppet. The height of the completed stair would measure about four feet. Now remember, the puppet's average height was 10-12 inches and the control rods extended beneath their feet about eight inches below stage. The lush historic spectacle of sweeping down the stairs would demand the operating rods be over four feet long! With loud laughter, everyone immediately recognized the impossible but voiced their enthusiasm for the stairs anyway. A compromise was reached by pre-setting the scene with Anna four steps up. Now one would think walking down four steps would not be much to crow about but in the hands of our resident diva, Lee George, with each step down, Anna injected a drama so regal it brought a hush to the audience. Understage our jaws dropped. Thank God four steps was the technical limit. I can only imagine the journey Lee would have taken with the scene without that boundary.

One of the big problems facing me in this production was reproducing the massive ancient Thai sculpture so omnipresent in all of my research books about Thailand. These images imparted the heavy sense of place – somber Buddhas, nubile temple dancers, enormous lotus flowers, and explicit erotic scenes of contorted orgasmic lovers. The last, of course, was forbidden to our stage but I knew I had to have the Buddha, the dancers, and lots of lotus blossoms. I began searching the antique and second hand shops which abounded on North State Street, and along Dearborn and Clark streets. Luck was with me as I first found an old lamp, its bulb held aloft by a Siamese temple maiden. The lotus blossoms proved to be plentiful as small bowls, ashtrays, and decorative plates were all over China Town. And Buddha, of course, was everywhere. My biggest decision was which one to choose. The lamp I, of course, destroyed and from the maiden made two dozen plaster copies. To save time, I bought about fifty assorted size lotus flowers and sprayed them all a flat white before affixing them to the plywood set to be redone and aged to look like stone. Buddha, however, did not make it to the spotlight. The front office told Luis they were unwilling to risk any religious controversy which might result from the use of his image in a theatrical presentation. I was pissed but the entire production had by that time so consumed me, I shrugged and plowed ahead. The plaster cast copies of the dancer had proved a very big chore. And gluing them to the set even more. The fact one completed palace wall panel weighed two tons was particularly distressing. They were 4' x 8' three quarter plywood outfitted with 2' x 4' sliders which fit into the stage tracks and glided on stage from the wings. The dancers and some of the lotus blossoms were attached on side mouldings to complete the ancient temple walls – two on each side of the stage. Gorgeous when finally placed and lit, but their beauty stood in sharp contrast to the gripes they elicited from anyone who had to handle them. Which meant everyone. Throughout the show, everybody had, at one time or another, a tech task with one of the walls. Luis defended me from the grouching but in private I admitted to him I had miscalculated how heavy the damn things would be.

The very last touch of magic was the addition of an actual water fountain for the heart of the enchanted secret garden where the two young lovers in the story meet. I was surprised no one raised any objections. No snide remarks were made about borrowing a mop from housekeeping. Everyone seemed to instinctively recognize a real water element in this scene would indeed be magical. The only resistance came from the front office who didn't want to put out the money to buy the needed miniature pump. After a few days and probably a meeting with Tom, the OK was given and all I had to do was find the damn thing. Finally an outfit who manufactured garden sculpture and decorative fountains filled the need. Coincidentally the place was a half block from Luis's apartment on Erie at Wells. The grumbling about the heavy scenery evaporated when everyone understage heard the "oohs", "aahs", and gasps from the audience as each new scene was revealed under Luis's and Tom's moody lights. David Traversa, of course, had outdone himself in making the beautiful costumes. Roy's contribution, though not bad, only succeeded in creating an unbalanced effect when their designs were onstage in the same scene. Luis and Tom certainly noticed, but neither said a word. Roy was happy to have his name listed on the program and at last there was some measure of peace backstage. This production sparkled like a drag queen on Halloween. Everyone was pleased.

Drama was, however, rarely totally absent at the Miniature Grand Opera. And the next episode not only created a shaking in the Green Room but an earthquake in me. Suddenly there appeared in our midst a slight muscular youth with light brown curly hair and green eyes named Rand Bohn. It was unusual for anyone beyond the theatre staff to have access to the Green Room but this kid just magically began hanging around before curtain and a few times even took a seat on an empty stool understage. He was not unknown to Luis, Lee, and Tom. Apparently he was the ex-boyfriend of a puppeteer who had left the theatre before my arrival. The reason he was hanging around was he wanted a job in the theatre. The trouble was, most of the guys backstage did not want him to have a job in our theatre. He elicited malicious gossip the moment he left the room. At first I attributed this to his good looks and the tension it introduced in our tight little circle. He was very sexy and what the gay community called butch. He stood out in an unwelcome way. The one rampant thing backstage in most theatres worldwide, but absent in ours, was sexual intrigue. Luis and David were lovers. The rest of us were sisters. Mr. Bohn really rocked our boat. And although I was slow to admit it, especially mine.

In retrospect, I realize a more threatening facet of Randy was his enormous experience with puppets outside of the Kungsholm. Here was a guy who had been making his own puppets since he was a kid. I eventually found he was known throughout the local puppetry scene and was a member of the national organization, the Puppeteers of America. He was talented and very experienced in most aspects of theatre production. The Kungsholm was the grand jewel of puppet theatres not just nationally but internationally. Rand wanted very much to be a part of it. The drama of his appearances went on for several months. It was interesting to watch how he slowly insinuated into the group.

He volunteered to do unpopular dirty work the others tried to avoid. Climbing the spiral stairs to the top of the fly loft to search out the scene drops for the upcoming show was one such job. There were layers of dust and dirt up there and one usually got pretty roughed up searching through the piles of sixteen foot long, rolled up canvasses. It was necessary to hang and unroll them at least a week before their show to inspect for any damage which might cause an accident once they went onstage. Repairs had to be made, smudges cleaned. A small tear, if not fixed, could easily suddenly rip and come crashing down on someone's unfortunate head once it was weighted. This was a job I enjoyed and usually cajoled someone into helping me. Miraculously, here was a guy who loved the backstage dirt as much as the backstage glitter. There were many such tasks at the Kungsholm.

So a butch dude like Randy eventually came to be seen as a plus. Pretty soon folk were teasing, "It's so nice to have a MAN around the house!" I don't remember how many months went by before Luis announced the front office had agreed to add Randy to the payroll. When he did, no one made a comment or rolled an eye. By that time he had become a part of the family. Distant, but still a part.

Curiously, the one thing Randy never adequately accomplished was a decent mastery of manipulating the Kundsholm puppets in performance. I can't say whether this was due to his lax discipline in rehearsing or other unknown. Most likely, time simply ran out. Unbeknownst to everyone, he had joined us in what was to be the final year of the theatre. He kept himself very busy with a bushel of technical projects but rarely did I see him rehearsing with a puppet. And there was only one way to conquer our little twelve inch actors and that was with experience. Most of the guys backstage had been pushing puppets at the Kungsholm for at least five years. To catch up, I rehearsed my ass off as soon as I got in the door. Randy never complained he wasn't given a challenging role onstage.

He seemed content to command whatever minor character Luis assigned him. At first we assumed he was only interested in the technical stuff. This notion was soon dispelled as I got to know him better. In actuality he was an amazingly gifted artist. This was only dimly visible in his first few months at the theatre. It was, however, enough to allow him into my private domain on the fourth floor in the carpentry shop where I labored constructing the scenery for our new productions and sometimes repairing old. Except for Tom, who faithfully came up to take photographs when I was working on something new, rarely did anyone venture up to the fourth floor. Luis sometimes made the trip.

Initially I asked Randy to help me carry a large set piece in need of repair to the fourth floor workshop. There was no elevator and safely maneuvering a set up or down from the fourth floor could not be done alone. This trip was Randy's first time in the shop. He was intoxicated. As earlier described, the shop was a wood worker's dream. Every tool one could possibly imagine plus exotic machines I had to slowly decipher were in the room. Rand said he had no idea our shop was so well equipped. I asked him to help in positioning and guiding the piece of scenery through the table saw. He made a suggestion which made the whole process easier and that was the beginning.

Little did I suspect that my first lesson from a master puppet artist and technical theatrical genius had, without fanfare, just taken place. This was the man who, although five years younger than myself, would teach me how to make puppets. Not just puppets, but extraordinary puppets! But that was almost a year in the future.

16

THE announcement of our next new production left me reeling with excitement. Luis had called a meeting with Tom and myself in the lighting booth high above the theatre balcony. When he said we would be tackling a revival of Bizet's opera *Carmen*, I was shocked. Our repertory had been traveling away from opera and although it was engraved in marble on the front of the building and incised in the concrete four stories above the entrance, opera had been heard in our theatre less and less since I joined. The truth was, our Broadway productions were outselling our operas. Business was business and the front office always went for the bottom line.

So why were we going to do *Carmen*? "Window dressing," said Tom. Part of the attraction of the Kungsholm was its snob appeal. Its elegant building, the jewel-box theater and its outrageous chandelier, its prestigious location, and the fact it was known historically as the miniature grand opera. A one-of-a-kind phenomenon. Yet musically speaking, the minute Carol Fox initiated the Lyric Opera of Chicago, it had begun to lose the lovers of the classical canon. Up until then, except for occasional traveling productions and recitals, the Kungsholm was the city's main operatic stage. In those times, the managers of the divas, baritones, and tenors of the day lobbied feverishly to have their recordings heard in our space. Now people could hear the voices live with a real orchestra. We simply couldn't compete. The Lyric was now the third largest opera company in the U.S.

Bringing back one of the most beloved operas of all time, management thought, would not necessarily suddenly bring crowds to our box office but would be a wonderful news item. And frankly, the Kungsholm needed all of the good PR it could get. So *Carmen* was green lighted and now it was up to the theatre staff to deliver.

I knew at once this was going to be a gigantic challenge and not just for myself. The rehearsal of the opera in French was going to be one helluva movie! Luis, of course, would guide and drive us through it but the hours would be long and something of this magnitude was surely to be a mine field when it came to casting. Most likely Lee would be named Carmen and Luis, if for no other than to keep Lee from wrecking the part, would have to cast himself opposite as the doomed scorned lover. No one else had a strong enough technique to play those duets with Lee and match his intensity. Roy would have been foolish enough to try but he would have been eaten alive before the second note was voiced. David would be in ecstasy when it came time to do those wonderful period costumes full of flashing Latin heat and high boots. And as for me, well I had a rather peculiar unusual situation ahead of me. Some of the original *Carmen* sets were still in the theatre. They were stored in the third floor loft area up above the stage. And they were nothing short of magnificent. Along with the frescoed ceiling of Scarpia's chamber in *Tosca,* the old *Carmen* sets were hauntingly beautiful. I surmised they were probably built in the late forties or early fifties by the team of master carpenters and designers who once ran the shop that now hosted only one man, me.

It took Luis, Tom, and I, with help from Randy, quite a few hours to push, drag, and identify all of the disparate pieces which had been abandoned for at least eight or nine years. The overall color scheme of everything was a very dusty blue and gray. Ghostly beautiful is how I would describe them. Tom, of course, was our source of information and it was from him we learned everything was accounted for except the last act. Without a word, everyone knew I was going to have to design and build the missing chapter. From the git, Luis hastily told me I did not have to match my design with the existing acts. "Do whatever you want Gary, I trust you," he said.

I knew the last act traditionally took place in front of a bullring and all I could think of at the moment was, "My gosh I'm gonna have to build a bullring!" I was beside myself with anticipation and excitement long before I sat down to sketch out the entire scene.

I don't remember actually asking Randy to help out, but before long everyone in the Green Room was teasing me about my new assistant. I have always been an artist in the romantic sense that I prefer to work alone and to do EVERYTHING myself. Allowing Randy to enter my space, I now understand, was a complicated act of altruism, respect for talent, and lust. If he had not been on the scene, I certainly would have built the damn set, as I had all the others, alone. As usual I did a fair amount of research before settling on what exactly I was going to put on the stage.

Luis' comment to do whatever I wanted was just his way of setting my imagination free. He knew how uptight I got when faced with a new production. But I also knew to totally disregard the atmosphere of the first acts was not the road to follow. The vintage sets were

Cardboard model for salon set,
4th act of *Carmen*.

breathtaking and for continuity, whatever I did had to in some way echo them. Once I had sketched out my plan, I cut a tiny scale model in white poster board and presented it to Luis and Tom. They were so pleased, Tom suggested the model should be displayed in the theatre lobby as a promotional.

And so the process began. I went to the lumber yard to place my order. Delivery was always scheduled before 10 in the morning because it had to pass through the main lobby of the restaurant to get up to the shop. The luncheon guests who would be attending our matinee began arriving around 11:30. Usually the lumber crew carried the stuff up but when Randy asked if I'd need any help on that morning I said, Sure. He was already in the theatre when I arrived around 9:30 the next day.

As requested, the crew usually deposited the lumber on the landing just outside the double doors leading into the shop. This allowed me planning space to rearrange what was always a fairly complicated mess of remnants from the previous activity. Making room for a new project was part of the process. Needless to say,

Randy volunteered to stick around. So together we pushed and shoved one inch thick pieces of plywood, two by fours, one by twos, etc. into some semblance of order. We swept sawdust and moved a couple of the larger saws to accommodate my directions. Occasionally Randy would make a helpful suggestion and I'd say, "Yeah, why not." Working with him was very easy.

One o'clock was our call time in the theatre and so when the hands pointed in that direction, we headed downstairs. Luis was strict and the stage had to be completely ready by fifteen after the hour. Unless word came over from the restaurant to hold the curtain, the show always began promptly at two. Luis used to say, "The Met starts on time. So do we." To which someone would always reply, "Girlfriend pay me Met money."

If I was building a new show, I would always head up to the shop after the stage was struck and the fire curtain lowered. Usually I would stop in the kitchen and carry some coffee up with me in one of the Kungsholm's elegant china white cups edged with gold and the coat of arms of the kingdom of Sweden. Occasionally Randy would tag along and as the days flew by, his presence in the shop was more and more common. So were the cutting queen comments from the Green Room. By this time, although no one was sure, it was suspected that something might be going on. No open accusations were ever made. Randy was, after all, living with his boyfriend. My rapport with him was easily explained with him working in the shop. The comment that made me freeze, however, came from Luis understage just before the curtain went up on the 10:30 PM Saturday evening performance. Everyone was in their places and the overture had just ended. In that quiet space before the lights went up on the first scene Luis suddenly said, "It smells like sex under here tonight." I almost fell off my stool. No less than fifteen minutes before, Randy and I had had sex for the first time in the scenery storage room adjacent to the understage area. While we were going at it, we could hear Lee saying, "Where the hell are Randy and Gary?"

The performance that night was quite lively and I remember commanding my characters like never before. We were kids of the sixties. Just because we worked at the very establishment puppet opera in the most prestigious commercial area of Chicago did not mean we were immune to the aphrodisiacal vibe permeating the country. The physical affair with Randy proceeded in very irregular encounters. He was pretty attached to his lover and did not want to risk a blow-up or break up. This added dimension, though troublesome for both, eventually emerged as minor to the parts we were to play in each other's lives.

So sex was the background noise to the construction of the last act of Bizet's beautiful opera of rejection and murder. In our private scenario, Rand and I only indulged when Randy wanted to. Sometimes he would just hang out in the shop while I was working. If I needed help with some awkward lifting or positioning of the lumber he would pitch in but I never gave him any specific task to complete independently. He admired my design and said I had ingeniously used the available onstage space. The bullring was set upstage. Over its entrance I had cut a large rose filigree window more appropriate to a renaissance cathedral. Though strange, it nevertheless set a marvelous gothic tone to the scene. In my early days working in this shop, one of the tools I had discovered was a remarkable specialized kind of jig saw called a CutAwl. More precise than a scroll saw, it was capable of carving out incredibly intricate patterns in surfaces up to an half inch thick. From the evidence of vintage scenery pieces throughout the theatre, it had obviously been a favorite tool of the carpenters who built the Kungsholm sets. It was now my star piece of equipment and I used it without any excuse. As the bullring neared completion, we knew it was going to be quite a challenge to transport it down four floors to the theatre. Randy made a suggestion as to how I could trim it without destroying the design as it would be seen from the audience. Our interactions and our friendship slowly accumulated the feeling we had known each other for a very long time. In actuality it was only approaching a year.

At the time the Carmen set was completed, we were, however, in the middle of rough terrain. Essentially the battle was about sex, when, and how often, and who called the shots. Randy won and this both pissed me off and sent me into a melancholy which Luis noticed and immediately deduced the reasons. Miraculously no one else backstage seemed to be aware of the drama. It seems the care we both took to camouflage our dirty doings disguised the scent of scandal from the queens. However during this period the question/comment was frequently directed to me. "What's with you, Elvira? Come down from your tree."

So with great fanfare the set was finally finished and there was a full house booked for the opening performance. Even though this was the premiere of a new production, we still had only the one night to make the switch from the closing show to the new one. Economics must have called the tune in this outrageous schedule. The front office was not focused on getting the production on right. They just wanted it on time. That it would demand a nearly sixteen hour day/night from us and that we would have to open the show the next afternoon did not concern them in the least. They knew we would do it and we never failed.

The 4th act of *Carmen*.
The bullring with the rose window is towards the back, the salon is on the left.
The intricate filigree patterns echoed similar lacy designs in
old scenic fragments of 20 years earlier.

On change night everyone was eager for the curtain to come down. A minute after our smiling curtain call, everyone shifted gears. The queens suddenly became hulking cursing stagehands and grips. The activity was relentless as everyone knew a night like this usually held more than a few unexpected and unwelcome surprises. Scenery was dragged and shoved, drops were lowered with and without warnings, loose props had to be stored, and the current puppets were yanked from their tracks and hustled off to their cases while the new Carmen cast was carefully brought up into the wings amid lots of "oohs" and "aahs" over the gorgeous costumes. Except for the fact that where the bonafides would have used words like "motherfucker", one heard either "girl" or "Mary."

The last two jobs would be to transport the sets onto the stage and into the wings, followed by re-setting the lights. We usually took our traditional kitchen raid break around one am. And it was after this everyone headed upstairs in high excitement to fetch the new set. I distinctly remember Randy exhibited a high sense of pride as everyone entered the shop. I now understand that as he had witnessed the daily progress of the set's construction and assisted in its creation, he probably, at last, felt some degree of prestige over the queens who had initially rejected him.

Everyone lavished compliments and couldn't wait to get it downstairs and under the lights. The set did prove a bit difficult to manoeuver down the stairs but it was finally accomplished with patience and much teasing. At last we entered from the back of the theater and down the west aisle to hoist everything over the orchestra pit to the stage. It fit beautifully and my usual self-criticisms were immediately dismissed by Luis. Tom, of course, had congratulated me and had taken his photos earlier that afternoon in the shop. He would take more when it was onstage after the first matinee.

We probably left the theater around three or four in the morning. Luis didn't even have to ask everybody return by noon! Everyone knew what was at stake and most of us would be back by ten or eleven. We would not be surprised to find Luis and Tom already there!

If time permitted, and once the lights were set, Luis would try to run through the show. Not that we hadn't rehearsed it till we dropped, but this would be our first time making our entrances and exits with the scenery and no one wanted their dramatic exit turned into a nightmare by colliding with a tree. Of equal importance was the logistics and intricate dances to be made between scenes and acts – often in pitch black.

Everything had to have its exact off-stage spot in the wings for calculated and safe movement. We would not know for sure the running time of the show until the opening was over. That of course would change as we became more comfortable and efficient with the tech of the show.

Time did not permit. The old sets were particularly heavy and the queens complained. My new set demanded equal muscle plus precision and the queens complained even louder. Luis simply yelled, "Oh Mary, please girl. You're sweating, Miss Thing. Your mascara will run. Try it again." We were having a good time in the name of the deadline bearing down on us. Time ran out.

At one o'clock we had to stop, reset the stage and hope for the best. Tom consoled us he had seen a hundred premieres at the Kungsholm and they had all been disasters. The evening show, he said would be much better.

Tom was right. The matinee was not quite a hurricane but things did get a bit twisted as the tape rolled on. Most of the errors were clunks with the movement of the monstrous scenery. David and Luis had done a skillful job at editing the recording we used. The music filled the auditorium and blared from our understage speakers, inspiring audience and performers alike. Lee, diva that he was, wrenched a mind-boggling Carmen from his puppet and matched any woman who had ever strode the Met with the melodrama of the death scene. Luis underplayed his part as the heartbroken murderous rejected lover while I remember myself nervous but soaring as the proud matador. Personally I had finally reached a point of confidence in my manipulation technique. I was nowhere near as good as Luis and David but my focus on their hands and fingers during the past three years had paid off.

There was no party scheduled but word had come down from the office that we could order anything we wanted except alcohol from the kitchen for our dinner. Normally we had access to anything on the smorgasbord menu. Special top priced items like steaks and lobster, etc. were off-limits to our staff. Ironically we regularly gorged ourselves on caviar when we raided the refrigerators on change nights.

So Bizet's *Carmen* still brings Randy to my mind. It was this music that echoed through my mind as the two of us made our way through the density of young unguided and uncertain passions towards a friendship that would end shortly after the Kungsholm closed and miraculously reconnect ten years later in Los Angeles.

The first run of *Carmen* was intoxicating for everybody at the Kungsholm. It was rare for anyone from the restaurant side to ever watch a production in the theatre. Primarily because while we were performing, they were cleaning up after those who had just left their tables and preparing for the next guests. But they all found time to snatch at least one act of *Carmen*. They would either stand in the wings backstage or sit with Tom up in the lighting booth. After the house lights went down, they were allowed to take a seat in the balcony. We were duly congratulated as we passed through the kitchen every afternoon on our way to the theatre. The front office was pleased and had succeeded in wringing a few lines of publicity in the media. I don't think *Carmen* actually increased attendance in the theater. There were a few nights and afternoons when we were sold out but during our normal repertory runs, that was normal. Yet it was a classical feather in our cap and from management's point, proof they were indeed trying to honor the heritage of the place and not merely exploiting its history.

Closer to home, it is now obvious it was during the construction of *Carmen* that Randy and I fell into the odd friendship laced with restrained lust which would propel me ever more sharply into, shall I say, destiny. We had worked hand-in-hand and traded information and know-how I use even today. Not in our most spaced out imaginations could either of us have envisioned the events that would quickly overtake us and send us flying.

Gary's assistant in the scene shop,
Rand Bohn standing in front of the Carmen set.
When the Kungsholm closed, Rand taught Gary
the rudiments of making puppets. Together they
made a cast of characters and, for a very short time,
performed in nightspots around Chicago.

17

ABOUT five months passed before Luis and Tom called me again up to the lighting booth to discuss new programing. Warned ahead of time, I had for a week been fantasizing the choice of *Carmen* had meant we would continue on the path of reviving the magical operas which once had made the place famous. In particular I was hoping they would announce the next up would be *Tosca.* As mentioned, the Renaissance era frescoed ceiling of Scarpia's apartment was still almost perfectly intact and stored in the fourth floor shop. Imagine a miniature reproduction of the Sistine chapel and you'll have a good idea. This was not photographic process. Someone had actually hand painted these extraordinary scenes of nubile, scantily clad virgins, robust fierce near naked warriors, angels, and demons floating against billowy clouds, blue skies, and fantastic waterfalls. Like many other such original pieces in the house it was a minor masterpiece of miniature scenic design. A pity none of these things bore any signatures.

But my dream was to disintegrate forthwith when I heard Tom say, "OK, *Oliver* it shall be." Oliver? Oliver? But sure, why not? *Oliver* was a natural. A gothic heartbreaking story full of cherubic unfortunate children set in old London Town. It was a perfect economic choice. I never knew whether it originated in the front office or Tom had set the ball to spinning.

I kept forgetting the Kungsholm existed for only one reason. To bring prestige and money to the corporation who had purchased it towards the end of its glory days when its purpose was still the celebration of art. *Carmen* had indeed just been part of management's plan and now it was back to what really brought in the theatre parties and the bucks. It had already been put on the schedule and set to open in three months. Hold on to your hats girls. Here we go again.

So although disappointed, I could already feel the adrenaline rushing as I contemplated the adventure of building the streets and alleyways of old London. The story provided ample reason for the decor to rage about the stage in typical grand gilded Kungsholm tradition. London Bridge! Big Ben! Buckingham palace! A dark alley behind Picadilly Circus! But for the biggest surprise, no one backstage was in the slightest prepared. I announced to Luis I was going to let Randy design the set! Just how this idea came into my head I cannot say. All through the building of *Carmen* Randy had made suggestions, some helpful and some not. Most of them I rejected and confined him to the role of assistant. I recognized his talent but still considered myself in charge if not a tad more talented than he. The sexual component of our relationship, though very tentative, exerted complications. Luis immediately responded I was sacrificing myself to help Randy get ahead. I don't know. He also told me that inasmuch as I ran the scene shop, I was free to do as I liked but he could not raise Randy's salary. Randy could do the design but he would continue to be paid a puppeteer wage. He also cautioned all responsibility would be on me and I would have to oversee the project closely, regardless of who authored it. I agreed to everything he said but still had to face Tom Doyle.

Tom's take was similar to Luis'. He said he'd seen similar scenarios and reminded me, for the first time, the Kungsholm would not last forever and I should be accumulating all of the design credits within reach while they were available. He said I had to think about my future. Yikes! If I had had even a microscopic idea of the explosions about to take place. He gave me his blessing and said he would be watching. In the Green Room that afternoon before the matinee, Luis told the staff *Oliver* would be our next production. Everyone was pleased and duly excited. Lee George's eyes sparkled as he talked about the famous love song the female lead sings, "As Long as He Needs Me." He was already visualizing his moves on stage. He was forever our diva.

After the matinee, I asked Randy to meet me in the shop to help take inventory of the lumber left over from *Carmen* and to plan what might be needed to build *Oliver* once the design was completed. I recall the joy we both expressed when I told him I was going to let him design the set for the new show. We, of course, played our expected roles, him jumping up and down with excitement and me calmly giving him the facts and conditions of the assignment, including no extra pay. He responded the money didn't matter and thanked me a thousand times over. I gave him a deadline to deliver drawings and repeated I would be working alongside him.

While all of this was going on, it seems the universe was simultaneously preparing me for cataclysmic events just around the corner. In 1970's Chicago, an artist living in a loft was a rare thing. Strangely there were tons of abandoned and shuttered factory buildings and warehouses everywhere in the city. All empty. Spaces like these were coveted in New York City but current laws and midwestern culture actively discouraged their creative use in Chicago. Not until the eighties did real estate developers wise up to the gold mines that had been dormant on their doorsteps for so long.

It is said there are no accidents in the universe. But one helluva coincidence had occurred at my place on St. James. The storefront I lived in illegally was divided in half. The street space facing the plate glass was a gallery of my paintings, and carved wood chess pieces, in the back was my workshop and bed. The tiny bathroom with a sink, a toilet and no hot water. I liked to think the front as no frills, Left Bank, artist elegant. Later I met people who remarked they had often passed but never found the place open. This was the height of my time at the Kungsholm when I left in the morning and didn't return home until midnight or much later if working on new set construction. One person, however, was determined to get a closer look. He had been so struck by one of the paintings inside, he had brought his wife, Della over to take a peek. She too was smitten and they slipped a number into the mailbox to call. I dialed and a week later two very bright, energetic people about my age knocked on the door.

The painting that interested them was a huge double canvas. Each piece 4' x 6'. It was part of my inequality in America series. It was stated in seventeen vaguely square-like shapes in mustard and yellow against a field of dark brown. The sixteen were positioned in flat diluted acrylic on one canvas but the seventeenth was alone on the other surface in the same colors but deeply impasto straight out of the tube. They asked, "How much?" My typical timid response when confronted by dollars connected with art was I'd think about it and call them. But scarcely a few days passed and Tom called me. He and Della had just hit upon a great idea. They owned a building downtown and the top floor was vacant. It seemed to them my gigantic canvases were beginning to crowd my little studio and just maybe I might want a bit more room. He gave me the address and said he'd drop the keys in my mailbox. Take a look at my leisure.

The entire top floor of a five story former munitions factory at 617 West Fulton Street in downtown Chicago! 3,800 square feet of open space! Four small beams supporting the roof were evenly placed down the middle but that was it. High wide windows about a foot apart stretched across the north and east side of the building allowing light galore! Chicago's magnificent skyline in my face three blocks away.

Five flights up the front and a rickety roofless old freight elevator opening directly into the space at the rear side of the building. No toilet or shower. No water at all! A ladder built against the south wall and heavy trap door led onto the roof. The floors were rough but fairly even. No heat. At the time, except for the bustling meat packing/storage district two blocks west and the fruit and vegetable market two blocks south on Randolph, the area was dominated by abandoned warehouses and gigantic empty manufacturing structures. The train yard a few paces northeast provided sparse unpredictable movement but the rumbling regularity of the Lake Street El one block south reminded me civilization was near, in spite of the spooky desolation of the terrain. A once-viable industrial district was now a ghost town, especially at night. What one then quaintly referred to as hobos slept in some of the boxcars in the train yard. And over this surreal and barren neighborhood one scented something quite unbelievable. At first whiff it was baffling, but then – my gosh, the unmistakably aroma of fresh chocolate! One felt as though one was swimming in it! The chocolate factory responsible was two blocks away. I wonder if it's still there? The area was literally on the doorstep of the Loop. Close enough for me to walk to the Kungsholm over on North Michigan or to Sears & Roebuck on State Street. This was a dream loft. Solitude. Challenging.

If I wanted it, all I had to do was deliver the painting as the first five month's rent. I sat alone in the windowsill at the north end of the building and watched a thousand scenarios parade. Could I really fill all of this space with my dreams? Dare I even try? Across the street loomed the vacant windows of the block long, block wide ten story former Sears warehouse. It was empty when I arrived and still mostly empty when I left five years later. It was late afternoon and I had to get back to the theatre for the evening performance. Very quietly I said yes to something inside of me, locked the door as I left and hurried down the five steep flights of dingy steps.

When I got to the Kungsholm, I used the pay phone just outside of the Green Room to call Tom and Della. The deal was struck and I delivered the painting to their apartment in the sky in a very stylish and new high rise overlooking Lincoln Park at the corner of Clark and Armitage. Tom ran a small construction company and Della worked part time in their business office. They had been high school sweethearts and grew up together in the same Italian immigrant neighborhood which ran along Blue Island Avenue on Chicago's South Side. They were gregarious, highly social and threw a lavish hanging party for friends to meet the artist of their new acquisition. Most of the people at the party seemed more intrigued I worked at the Kungsholm than interested in my painting. Tom, Della and I took to each other from the git. We had great fun together and inhaled. Our friendship would continue to grow over the years.

Moving the entire contents of an artist's studio is no joke. Especially if three quarters of the works are outsized four by four, five by five, or six by six foot canvases, heavy floor mounted electrical saws, and a cast cement water spewing garden fountain measuring four by five feet and weighing a ton! Luckily I had easy access to a group of girls, I mean guys, who had years of experience of tackling all manner of delicate problems of transport. Everyone backstage was excited and curious about my move and agreed to help on the next Monday. Mind you, Monday was our only day off.

I rented a truck and with the usual synchronized affectionate bitching and yelling, we loaded up to capacity. Luis, of course, assuming his normal place directed what went on first. Soon someone lobed the comment we weren't in the theater and he had better shut his trap and start lifting a few things himself. We all laughed. Curiously this was the only time in the entire three years I knew these guys that we were together outside of the theater. Yet the same dynamic that bound us at the Kungsholm translated seamlessly in this totally different setting. I'd surmise we were actually no different than any other performing company when they were on tour. We had to make a second trip to dismantle and load the cement fountain which proved a task as difficult as moving the bullring in Carmen. It really did weigh close to ten tons! Luis, however, stage-managed everything and, as usual, his directions got the job done!

The only person in our group I saw outside of the theater was Randy. And that was not very often. Usually our connections revolved around quick sex at the storefront before I moved. Never on our day off. Yet our personal relationship slowly grew in the soil of our unique relationship inside the theatre. He delivered his sketches for *Oliver* shortly after I completed my big relocation. I approved them and showed them to Luis and Tom who surprisingly made no critical comments. We were set to calculate the lumber needs and place the order.

During this short interlude, another development occurred that would draw Randy and myself even closer together. He had begun to have a rocky time with his lover Chuck. Passing my old storefront and noticing it was still vacant, he asked if I would help him get the lease on it. This involved me contacting the leasing agent to recommend Randy as the next tenant and co-signing the lease as Randy was short a few months of his twenty-first birthday. With obvious ulterior motive, I cinched the lease over the telephone and went with Randy to sign. Much to my dismay, he and Chuck reconciled a few weeks later. Unbeknownst to me, however, my old studio on St. James Place would shortly resume its role as a class room where I would learn skills of paramount importance to this very day.

Randy continued to live with Chuck but immediately got busy turning his new space into a creative workshop of his own design. One of the first things he did was to demolish the ten feet off the floor platform where I slept and rebuild it in the exact same measurement but with different wood joint techniques. I guess I was still attached to the place because this annoyed me until I realized it was his way of taking possession. He also tore down the partition separating back from front and rebuilt it with the addition of wheels making it movable.

Meanwhile back at the theatre, another bizarre twist had just taken place. We were suddenly invaded by two straight men and a woman! Everyone tried their best to be accepting but they were outsiders from the moment they arrived. All three were music students at DePaul University in downtown Chicago. One of the music professors also happened to be a Kungsholm fan. It was his idea to place some of his students at the puppet opera as apprentices in a professional musical environment. He didn't waste time calling the Kungsholm but made direct contact with the owner corporation, the Fred Harvey Company. Soon Luis was called into the office and told to make room for John, Stephen, and Lois! Tom felt the front office had seen an opportunity for a public reaffirmation of the cultural importance of the Kungsholm and not any less valuable – more publicity.

Whatever the reasons in the office, it was the backstage staff who had to make adjustments. The three newcomers were mere college kids and totally unprepared for the rough ballistic movement powering our operation. It was like dumping twelve year old ballerinas into a stripper joint. Luis assigned each of us time to teach them the basics of operating the puppets. He let us know we would be paid. We balked. No one had taken time to teach any of us a damn thing. It was all "Get it from the wings, baby, or get the hell out!" Eating in the Green Room, a gladiator arena of raunchy banter, camp, and hilarious put-downs, became as silent as a hospital lunchroom. No one was having any fun. No one was being themselves. Of course the kids had no idea how to behave and mostly segregated themselves at one end of our long table. Finally Luis took hold of the situation and broke the ice with a torrent of high queen vernacular worthy of the Paris Opera, La Scala, or the Met. The room froze until Roy responded in kind. Nearly undetectable laughter slowly grew into a roar and suddenly everything returned to normal. I guess at some unconscious level we had all agreed if the kids were to learn anything from us, it would have to be in our authentic environment. We certainly couldn't duplicate the lecture halls at DePaul or even the backstage goings on at a student production.

 All three of them seemed to understand and although Lois and Stephen still tended to separate themselves, John jumped on the wagon but not into bed with anyone of us, as far as I know. Once they had mastered a modicum of manipulation technique, Luis gave them very small chorus responsibilities in each show. One place rich in learning opportunity was the tech at onstage level. Quite different from the tech understage, which usually cross referenced one's attention between puppet operation and moving set pieces simultaneously. Easy if one had four hands, otherwise a tricky business. Onstage, however, one had to be aware of everything going on understage even though one had zero visibility. One had to know what and where something was going on, when it going to change and how fast. What came next? Which drop to raise and which drop to lower? Which puppets needed to change tracks and which new puppets needed to be placed into a track, while removing others to the wings. And most important, on what note of the music should the red velvet curtain be raised or lowered and at what speed. How to avoid rope burns? To this day I can't figure out why none of us wore gloves when doing onstage tech. All three kids eventually became fairly adept at onstage tech. To Luis' delight, he didn't have to drill them with the music cues. For us oldtimers, the music could sometimes cause a few explosions. But as these were music students and Luis had played a New York City recital, he spoke to them as musician in the language of musicians – as foreign to us as the Spanish he sometimes fell into speaking with David Traversa.

Of course all of these wild changes, both inside and out of the theatre, exerted varying degrees of influence and consequent drama in the daily life of the puppet opera.

And just when it seemed this goulash was quietly simmering and beginning to smell quite delicious, an unexplainable ominous force field seemed to descend. Usually most of the high jinx of the Kungsholm could be traced to the volatile energies raging in the opera house. The restaurant seemed to run smoothly unless there was a large party booked in which some of the guests were local celebrities. Soon, however, some of us began to be aware a threatening force was silently pacing throughout the entire institution. A rumor had started to circulate the Harvey Corporation was selling the place and we would either close or experience drastic reorganization. I'm not sure what the thinking was in the restaurant but we in the theatre brushed it off like a tiny insect. The Miniature Grand Opera was an acknowledged cultural landmark internationally known in a city that traditionally played second fiddle to the royalty of New York. This was something Manhattanites could never rival. Other world class puppeteers, Bill Baird for one, might make Greenwich Village their home, but even such a genius as he could never reproduce the grandeur of our productions, let alone the magnificence of our surroundings. We were a high cultural institution. Untouchable. Admired.

But the rumors continued to intensify. Randy and I met up in the wood shop and inventoried all of the lumber currently on hand. Carefully reviewing his *Oliver* plans and sketches, we made a list of what would be needed to build the bridge over the River Thames, the silhouette of St Paul's Cathedral, and the gates leading into Buckingham Palace. Such a set this was going to be. I could see Randy was straining at the starting gate, eager for the gunshot to release what, for him, must have been a long awaited creative moment. This was his big chance, his first professional credit. I saw myself in him and felt a chill that I could give him this opportunity even though the energy between us was increasingly, shall I say, less than I desired. Damn desire, damn it! Constantly setting one off balance and blanketing everything with doubt. But I had made my choice and at bottom knew it had been the right one. I would pick up the next show after *Oliver* premiered, Tom had already mentioned *Fiddler on the Roof*. An acknowledged considerable percentage of our faithful audience was historically Jewish. We were surprised the front office had not already suggested it.

The rumors. Slowly much of the talk in the Green Room was about the rumors. Needless to say, we would be losing much, much more than a job in a restaurant.

Waiter, maitre'd, manager, pastry chef – all of which could move across town to another eatery. There was nowhere across the entire globe we could go. Far, far, far fetched. The Salzburg Marionette Theater performed *The Barber of Seville* and *The Magic Flute.* But marionettes? The other side of the Atlantic Ocean? If any this rumor was true, we were all, quite without a question, fucked. And true to our treatment at the Kungsholm, very, very royally. Not one queen would face the guillotine but several! And certainly not stepping up onto the platform head held high but instead screaming and cursing.

When Randy and I walked over to the lumberyard to place our order, we were dumbfounded when the office told us the Kungsholm invoices had been paid in full and the account closed! Surely they were mistaken. They assured us they were not. They were sorry to lose the account and asked us where management was shifting its business. This was the thread of hope Randy and I silently carried on our way back to the theater.

Luis had not yet returned from the break between the matinee and evening performance and Tom was nowhere to be found. We decided to get busy with the wood that was upstairs. We reasoned all of this confusion would eventually sort itself out but the one certainty before us was we had a show to build and every day counted. Understandably, Randy was impatient and wanted to hear steel slicing through wood. The smell of the saw dust would calm us both down.

When we went downstairs at six to grab a bite before setting the evening stage, everybody was already chattering away in the Green Room. Luis was there but not Tom. Luis said he was surprised and didn't know anything about it, he would ask Tom before he made any inquiry up in the office. He'd let us know tomorrow.

The answer tomorrow brought was less than encouraging. Yes, the account had indeed been closed. And for the moment the production of *Oliver* was to be postponed. I saw Randy's eyes flicker in alarm. They said *Oliver* would be replaced on the schedule with *Camelot.* News would be forthcoming. Relax. Shit!

Everybody in the room heard the conversation and like a chorus, responded with, "What do they mean, relax?" "What the fuck is going on?" "Relax about what?" "Goddamnit!" Luis made a stab at calming the hoards but the tension of the past months had grown to proportions unsuspected by all of us. The uproar was suddenly interrupted when Tom voice from the lighting booth came over the intercom, "Hey you guys, what's going on? It's almost seven thirty and the stage still isn't set. What's the deal?"

Heretofore, at seven sharp like Westpoint cadets, we simultaneously converged on and under the stage to prepare for the evening performance. A silent theatrical ritual, the only words spoken aloud asking if anyone was trading roles or tech. With Luis' approval, we often traded responsibilities at the last minute. And depending on the trade, puppets would be set accordingly. If the entrance was directed for stage right, some divas preferred the first track and some swore by the third. A small difference but understood, respected and always honored. I preferred the first or the second, never the third. The third track always left me with a stiff neck.

Tom's voice caused our eyes to dart back and forth and in a second the loud noise of chairs pushing back from the table filled the room. Everyone snapped back into the present moment and headed for the stage. Once completed, everyone seemed to head in a different direction. Whoever had usher duty went into the locker room to change into their red jacket and black trousers, a few of us went to the kitchen to get coffee, Luis went up to the light booth to talk to Tom. Back in the Green Room, no one had much of anything to say. Compounding the unwelcome news we'd just heard, everybody just seemed tired. The attendance in the theater had been unusually full that week. Large audiences are a guarantee the performers will bust their butts responding to the energy out front and we were no different. Someone went onstage to take a peek through the curtain and came back with the news it looked as though we were going to have another fairly full house. It was probably exactly what everyone needed to hear and the best medicine for the gloom that had suddenly dropped.

When Luis came down from talking with Tom, everyone immediately deluged him with questions. But Tom didn't know anything more than we did. We would just have to wait. In a few minutes Luis disappeared understage to check the tape and called places. Without a word, we scattered. Even though there was a tense thick feeling understage, the performance unfolded beautifully. Emotionally full and suspenseful. No surprise there. This was our natural arena to allow our insides free range. As I left the theatre that night, the lonely lightbulb hanging in the middle of the dark stage casting its weird shadows no longer seemed poetic. It was ominous and totally without its usual hint of theatre magic.

And yet as I hit the street, I was uplifted. It was one of those great warm spring evenings in Chicago and I headed off towards my new loft. The novelty of walking back and forth to the theatre was still a lot of fun. I could either cross the river over the Michigan Avenue bridge and amble west along Wacker Drive past all the skyscrapers, or more adventuresomely zigzag through the side streets north of the river and cross the dangerous looking bridge behind the gigantic Merchandise Mart. The Mart route had a sense of threat. The four-story buildings in its shadow were some of the oldest in the city and the streets were very dimly lit. Unlike busy Wacker, there was rarely any traffic. The Kinzie Street bridge led me directly into the train yard and silent emptiness, but also into the sweet atmosphere of the chocolate factory. The occasional lone figure never looked my way and I returned the favor. Couldn't beat it under a full moon and hot night. This was my favorite path.

I had more of a sense of the metropolis if I travelled Wacker which I loved, but going that way I also had to endure the nerve shattering experience of walking the Lake Street Bridge with the El noisily grumbling and shaking the shit out of everything. If I was on the bridge and heard the El approaching I'd run to get the hell off the bridge before it got there. Nothing romantic about that. Once I reached my deserted street and my building, I usually bounded up the five flights.

Walking home these days, however, I seemed to be walking side by side with an invisible companion. This guy chattered on and on about how he was beginning to see my future. I'd calmly tell him all of his speculations were way off the mark but he'd insist I pay attention. He said a very big change was coming.

The very next day as we, one at a time, made our usual entrances into the Green Room carrying a cup of coffee or a snack we'd snatched passing through the kitchen, we all later agreed we'd felt it. We couldn't have identified what it was, but it was without a doubt in the room. Tom called down on the intercom and asked Luis if everyone had clocked in. A few minutes later he came in his snow white hair peeking from his usual baseball cap. He was carrying a cup of coffee. Without sitting down or undue ceremony he calmly announced Mr. Madsen had informed him the Kungsholm would be closing within a week! Not just the theatre, but the entire operation. Hopefully we would at least know a day ahead of time.

One could have heard the beating of butterfly wings. One sensed tragedy and heaviness. We all felt immense sorrow and irreplaceable loss. The end of a grand theatrical institution, a unique international cultural landmark was staring at the hangman's noose and we were the unlucky witnesses. Someone said, "Shit!" But no one reacted or laughed. Everyone seemed to realize this was not Hollywood and there would be no last minute rescue. Our legs would wildly spasm and then dangle in utter despair. Immediately afterwards there was some light conversation and questions but as it was already one thirty, we quickly dispersed to meet the matinee at two. The bomb consequently detonated after the show was over.

"What had happened?"
"Was the place being sold?"
"Would the theatre be reorganized and continue?"
"How could the Kungsholm just close?"
"Weren't people aware of its history?"
"Could the Chicago Symphony just close?"
"What the fuck was going on?"

These and a thousand other questions ricocheted across the stage as we struck it after the matinee. No one asked about unemployment. As a matter of fact, no one seemed at all worried about their personal future. The concern among the vets and myself focused on the theatre. At some level we were well aware of the cultural importance of the Kungsholm puppets and their environment of master craftsman settings. What would become of them?

A thousand questions. And none of us were connected into the remotest circuit that could sympathetically find the answers. Our powerlessness was reflected in our behavior the next few days. No one suggested a plan of any sort to delay the avalanche bearing down above us. We continued our duties as if nothing out of the ordinary was afoot. When the fateful day arrived, we were still doing *Camelot*. And how odd, I thought to myself. *Camelot* had been playing on the night David Pendleton had interviewed me for a job behind the historic footlights. Charles Wilson had fetched me from the royal box where I had been seated me on arrival and took me backstage through the auditorium stage left door. I was practically numb that night. It was the beginning of my adventure in puppetry and I was stepping across a milestone. Now, three years later, I was again experiencing numbness at the Kungsholm but totally unaware I was moving over another milestone into a new adventure full of puppets.

When the performance ended that night, the audience had responded with sweet applause and the usual sudden audible in-breaths of surprise which always occurred when, after the puppets had taken their bows and the curtain fell, it rose again and the puppeteers stood up towering over the set like giants! After years of seeing this, I was always impressed I too reacted with the same shock as the audience. One's brain had so adjusted to the scale of watching the puppets, the abrupt intrusion of reality never failed to surprise. Knowing the audience that night would leave the theatre unaware they had witnessed the final frame of decades of creativity, hard work, dreams, and joy was too painful for me to contemplate. Their returning home and telling friends and family to go and see the Puppet Opera would be futile.

We struck the stage as usual that night – removing the puppets from the tracks and leaving them in the wings as if we would be returning the next day to prepare for the matinee. Ten people unceremoniously said goodbye. Lois had long since left us and the program at DePaul which had placed her at the Kungsholm. David Tacorante, of late, was only intermittently a presence. Neither Tom, Luis, Lee, Donald, Roy, John, Stephen, Charles, Randy, or myself made any kind of formal gesture of farewell. We simply cleaned out our lockers and left the lonesome worklight shining dimly on the stage. A sad disgraceful moment for the cultural landscape of Chicago.

A year or so later an ill-informed display of Kungshom artifacts, puppetry, and mismatched scenery would be mounted semi-permanently at Chicago's Museum of Science and Industry and would remain in place for about fifteen years. That the powers would expend the energy and time to mount the exhibit is interesting because, to my knowledge, they did nothing at the time of the destruction. On rare occasion, an article would be published on the disappearance of the tiny jewel in the cultural landscape of Chicago. The most egregious, offensive, and poorly researched claiming in its last days, the Kungsholm had been robbed of many of its theatrical treasures. One big unfortunate piece of misinformation. I was there, no one took anything. The miracle is, as attached as some of us were to the place, our respect for it automatically precluded scavenging any souvenirs. Two items I would love to have today; the little red caboose I had built for the train station scene in *Gypsy.* At the end of the song 'Together,' all of the puppets pile onto the back of the caboose as it glides off into the wings. It was a tricky maneuver involving the usual challenge surmounting steps and Luis had at first vetoed it. I, however, forged ahead, built the caboose, and brought it down to the theater for everyone to see. We set it onto a track and Lee got a couple of puppets to make a test. It wasn't easy but everyone loved the effect and with practice there would be no problem. The caboose was in. The other piece would have been that darn glamorous Sistine ceiling from *Tosca.* Eight by four and weighing a ton!

"Camelot! Camelot!
In short, there's simply not
A more congenial spot
For happily-ever-aftering than here
In Camelot."

THE LYRICS from the Broadway production. *Camelot* was playing when I started at the Kungsholm. *Camelot* was playing when the Kungsholm closed. I cleared out my locker, and together with the other puppeteers put understage in order, neatly placed the Camelot puppets in their racks, set the ghost light centerstage and left just as if we would return the next day. The unspoken truth oppressed. No one would return. There would be no closure. No shared discussion of our grief, and certainly no joyous "wrap party" to celebrate a job well done.

We dispersed out into the night in a silent, almost solemn shared confusion. No one exchanged telephone numbers, no one said, "Let's keep in touch." Who were we, mere puppet artists of the Opera, to question what was happening to us? Like Madama Butterfly we should just kill ourselves because of our helplessness. I would rather we act in the spirit of Tosca and plunge the knife into Scarpia. Then stand over him and groan in the voices of Callas and Price. "Die, die….die. You exploitive, selfish, greedy excuse for a man." Or a society. Or the supposedly culturally aware city of Chicago. Where the hell were the protest and concern of the so called civic and cultural leaders of the Second City? That's why you're called the Second City. This would not have happened in New York. Let alone Paris or Vienna.

 Luis and I walked together a fairly short distance towards our apartments. The others headed in the direction of their bus or subway stops. It was a bleak, bleak night and I was in a very dark mood. Luis and I simply nodded when I turned South and he headed up the steps of his place. Not a word.

The resilience of youth took over in the morning. I hopped the Clark Street bus and headed up to St. James Place, my old studio, now Randy's new studio. On past occasions we had bantered the idea of creating our own puppets and making a splash as a club act in Chicago's singles bar scene. We wasted no time marching to this new drum beat.

Neither of us even thought about looking for another job. We were under the spell of puppets that did not yet even exist! The energy was manic. We headed for the hardware store, the art supply, and happily to the lumber yard. In about two months we had six hand puppets, a classic ten foot tall stage with red velvet curtain and gold fringe, and a script for a raunchy *Punch & Judy*. Miraculously we convinced the owner of a nearby bar to let us strut our stuff. He would not pay us but we could keep any donations patrons might throw into the top hat! We performed for about a month and then everything collapsed. The landlords of our respective studios began knocking louder. And Chuck, Randy's partner, was raging with jealousy. The curtain came down. Another parting.

I opted for the quickest and easiest way to make some money. I got my chauffeur license and began cruising Chicago's downtown streets in a yellow taxi. About two months later Randy would surprise me at my loft to say he was moving alone to Los Angeles where he worked with the Bob Baker Marionette Theater for a short while before giving up puppets, he thought, for good. Amazingly we reconnected when I moved to Los Angeles in 1984. We had not seen each other for almost 14 years. In an odd twist, when he saw what I was doing with the puppets he had taught me to make, he was inspired to return to his first love and began immediately to create his own spectacular marionettes. Most unfortunately he was felled by the HIV-AIDS health crisis. I picked him up from the nursing home and took him for a ride in the mountains two days before he passed in 1986. He was 30, maybe 32, years old.

Out of the dynamic pool of puppeteers that made the Kungsholm so famous, with the exception of a few, most did not continue in the art after the puppet opera closed.

Bill Fosser had, however, kept moving with his usual tenacity. For a while he had been tapped to bring his Opera in Focus to Chicago's Museum of Science and Industry when the museum installed a semi-permanent exhibit of Kungsholm puppets and artifacts. A few years later, (1980-1982?) I learned he had signed a contract to perform on the top floor of the very popular French restaurant called, "The Magic Pan". This place was located on Oak Street in the same chic North Michigan Avenue district as the Kungsholm. In this setting Fosser had recreated the formula of the Kungsholm; an elegant meal and then the puppet opera!

I took a friend there for lunch and asked directions to the opera. I was directed through the kitchen and when I opened the door of the Green Room, I was shocked to be greeted by many of the same faces from the Kungsholm days. There was immediate pandemonium and shouts, "Elvira!" Hugs and a rush of questions before Fosser called 15 minutes and everyone dispersed to prepare for the show. In the room were Luis Tacorante, Lee George, and his brother Donald! Here we stood, 5 veterans of an internationally known theatre. Still pushing puppets. Our passion. What a reunion. It was the last time I saw Lee and Donald. A year later when Fosser had left "The Magic Pan," I encountered Luis, a wee bit tipsy, one late night coming out of our favorite bar not far from the Kungsholm. I remember he squinted and said, "Gary Jones?" I said, "Yes." We hugged and he vanished down the street.

There was a brief bizarre encounter with Charles Wilson handing out towels at a bath house, also in the same posh neighborhood of the Kungsholm. It seemed although we had scattered, we somehow stuck close to what had been our second cherished home. We chatted for a moment but there was a line forming behind me.

Finally and even more strangely I answered the telephone one night (1982) to find my gentle nemesis Roy Slocum on the other end of the line. Cordial and friendly he had recently read a newspaper article about me and my Blackstreet USA Puppet Theatre and just wanted to congratulate me. The conversation went on for longer than I expected as we attempted to catch up. He did not know the whereabouts of any of our puppeteer comrades. He was now employed with Lufthansa Airlines as the American "fixer" for their German employees working transatlantic flights. We laughed lots and hung up. We did not discuss the Kungsholm. A mirror of our behavior on the last night of performance at the puppet opera. Still not enough years had passed to speak of the pain, separation, and confusion? Why?

Looking back it has been nearly 60 unbelievable years since I first stepped into that magnificent jewel box echoing the great opera houses of the world, 48 years have passed to mark when the small profiteers locked those doors, and 43 annual calendars now celebrate my own Blackstreet USA Puppet Theatre. My puppets have dragged me to Iceland, Germany, Holland, Portugal, Japan, Mexico, Honduras, and India. The American stops in-between the international tours are far too many to list. Because of the controversial sculpture of my African American figures I have been praised and damned. Most commercial doors slammed tight. I am fairly immune to all of it.

I wrote these pages to remind people of the validity and beauty of their passions. Their own personal Camelots. Contained therein is the original fire. May you do whatever is necessary – fan it, toss gasoline on it, dance around it – to coax it into a poetic life giving blaze. When it becomes unbearably white hot and you start to sweat, then you will know what it was like to see the great chandelier fade to black, to feel the rush of air as the red and gold curtain parted, to hear the first bars of the sublime historic music. Then you will know what it felt like to be understage at the Kungsholm Miniature Grand Opera of Chicago.

                                                        Gary Jones
                                                        Los Angeles, California
                                                        August, 2018

Gary Jones is an interdisciplinary sculptor, puppet artist, and writer. His vision is expressed in paint, fibre, bronze, fabric, wood, resin, movement, and the English language. For four years he was the scenic designer at Chicago's internationally acclaimed Kungsholm Miniature Grand Opera. After the theatre closed in 1971, Gary established Blackstreet USA Puppet Theatre and has toured throughout the U.S. and internationally. Forever looking forward, he continues to explore his unique movement language exploiting the barrier between the real and the unreal, the finished puppet and the unfinished puppet artist.

www.ingramcontent.com/pod-product-compliance
Lightning Source LLC
Chambersburg PA
CBHW060515300426
44112CB00017B/2675